The
Aperture
Effect

Praise for *The Aperture Effect*

"Dr. Ford's book is a profound contribution to integrating mindfulness into our daily lives. With clarity and insight, she guides us step-by-step in using present moment awareness as a powerful, reliable path to healing and deepening our relationships. Her writing is infused with the wisdom that the challenges we face in our most important connections are opportunities for growth, transformation, and greater love."

—Shauna Shapiro, PhD, professor and
author of *Good Morning, I Love You*

"Dr. Ford takes you on a journey that simplifies the enormous complexity of loving and being loved. She brings hope to every struggling marriage. With wisdom and heart, she guides you to learn together, grow together, and discover the hidden treasures that only the hard work of commitment to love can reveal."

—Ellyn Bader, PhD, cofounder of the Couples Institute and
cocreator of the Developmental Model of Couples Therapy

"An aperture—a window or a lens—allows for the passage of light. Dr. Ford applies this metaphor to awareness, openness, and vulnerability in ourselves and others in the service of intimate relationships. Her strategies include mindfulness, patterns of interpersonal dynamics, and self-reflection to bring couples to deeper levels of interpersonal connection. The reader will find her practical and insightful guidance through the challenges of relationships both enlightening and useful. Highly recommended for therapists, couples, and anyone in any kind of relationship."

—Louis Cozolino, PhD, author of *Why Therapy Works*

"Balancing neurological research with emotional potential, *The Aperture Effect* is an immersive and accessible relationship guide."

—*Foreword* Clarion Reviews

"At first glance, *The Aperture Effect* appears to be a book about couples—but it's really a book about relational intelligence. Kathryn Ford introduces 'aperture awareness' as a powerful way of attuning to openness between people—an attunement that shapes how we connect, learn, and adapt together. Learning here is not abstract; it's embodied—in the rhythm of breath, in the pauses between words, in the decision to stay present when it would be easier to turn away. As someone who has spent a lifetime exploring how we learn and innovate, I'm struck by the humility and clarity of this work. *The Aperture Effect* doesn't simplify complexity—it gives us tools to move within it. In a time of fragmentation and distraction, this book invites us back to the relational field, where change—personal and shared—actually begins. It offers no quick fixes but something better: a way to pay attention that can change everything."

—John Seely Brown, former chief scientist of Xerox Corporation

The
Aperture
Effect

**A RADICALLY SIMPLE APPROACH
TO FINDING JOY AND CONNECTION
IN YOUR RELATIONSHIP**

Kathryn Ford, MD

GFB

Published by GFB™, Seattle
www.girlfridayproductions.com

Produced by Girl Friday Productions

Cover design: Emily Weigel
Production editorial: Katherine Richards
Project management: Emilie Sandoz-Voyer

Image credits: cover © iStock Photo/adaask

ISBN (paperback): 978-1-964721-63-7
ISBN (hardcover): 978-1-964721-93-4
ISBN (ebook): 978-1-964721-62-0

Library of Congress Control Number: 2025906950

First edition

For Peter

Contents

Prelude

1.

He admires the fresh flowers on the hall table. Nice.
She has a touch with such things.
He'll have to remember to tell her he likes them.
She comes in with bags of groceries.
He's going through the mail.
She says hi.
He says hi.
Later that night she minds that he didn't notice the flowers.

2.

You're trying to talk.
He's looking away, fidgeting, checking his watch.
You feel frustrated, defeated.
You no longer know how to reach him.

3.

I know I will never get tired of watching her sleep.
She is the one who satisfies
Some longing I've had since before everything
I now know about longing.
And still I know so little.

4.

He stops to pick up the dry cleaning, vaguely aware of wanting
To be appreciated for this contribution.

5.

What are the gaps between who I think you are
And who you are?

6.

The room feels airless.
Nothing is moving.
I think I'll go to the grocery store later.
She's looking at me. What did she say?
She's looking disappointed. Why?
She shrugs. Why?
Then I'm back in the kitchen, and she's driving away.
I feel lost.
What happened?

7.

What once seemed clean and shining is now
Cold, dark, and painful.

8.

Susan and Brian moved in together, planned to marry.
Then things began to unravel.
The more she tried to talk, the worse things got.
She understood him less and less;
She liked herself less and less.
Soon she became afraid to talk to him.
The only thing she knows is that
She loves him and he loves her,
Still.

9.

When did you stop meeting me at the door when I come home?
Was it before we married?
After?
Before we moved into the bigger house?
Or after?
Before I kissed Melissa, but you didn't know—or did you?
Or after?
Before we found out we couldn't have kids?
Or after?

10.

She looks up as the door closes behind him, feels sad.
Did he say goodbye? Maybe he's coming back to say goodbye.
Maybe he just took the garbage out? Was she distracted?

11.

There's that little thing she does with her lip
When she's thinking.
He thinks of it and smiles.

12.

He appears in the doorway just before bed,
Wearing those faded pajamas
That she used to hate, but now loves.
Tenderness overtakes her.

13.

He watches her cross the lawn,
Coming to him,
As she has for so many years.
Distracted, she doesn't see him sitting by the tree watching her,
Then she looks up and smiles.

Introduction

In relationships, the most important thing is what is happening right now, right here, inside us and between us. For more than twenty years, I've been helping couples find their way to loving each other better by paying attention to their openness, their *apertures*, to each other in each moment. And by teaching them how to use this *aperture awareness* to connect.

Couples come to me when they are just beginning or coming apart, angry, bored, hopeful, or hopeless. In all these moments, everything they want from each other depends on their ability to be aware of their openness and to know what to do to get open, reopen, stay open. And what to do to avoid injury when this isn't possible.

I came to Stanford for my psychiatry residency. At the time, Stanford psychiatry was pursuing two rich traditions: one, a medical approach understanding mental and emotional suffering as illness that must be treated, usually by physical interventions that increasingly involved medication; and the other, a psychodynamic approach, understanding suffering not as illness but as part of life, and amenable to change through a process of relationship and conversation. I was increasingly drawn to learning about suffering that is simply part of the challenges of life—challenges that require us to digest experience, sometimes difficult experience, and turn it into the next piece of our development.

During my residency, I was also eagerly immersing myself

in two other ways of understanding human experience: neuroscience and Buddhist psychology. The field of neuroscience was bursting with exciting new discoveries, expanding our understanding of the neurological basis for our experiences—including our suffering.

Researchers were discovering that this physical substrate, the brain, is endowed with far more ability to change, *neuroplasticity*, than we had previously thought. We were learning that our experiences shape and reshape our brains throughout our lives and that we can participate in these changes.

In choosing Stanford, and thus Northern California, for residency, I serendipitously landed among a wealth of teachings about yoga, Buddhism, and meditation.

Meditation and yoga were introducing me to the power of in-the-moment awareness, or mindfulness. I was learning how to train myself to be aware of what was unfolding in each moment. I was also starting to learn the benefits of this kind of attention and how it is different from what we usually do.

The wisdom of meditators, neuroscientists, and psychotherapists converged on a few very important ideas. We, and our brains, have certain biases and tendencies that influence how we feel, think, and behave, *and* we can shape those tendencies. Our capacity to learn throughout life and thus to revise our brains and our behavior is extensive, and we gain the ability to influence our brains, and our lives, through mindful attention.

I also began to notice the interesting similarity of the mindfulness I was learning—on the meditation cushion and on the yoga mat—with the kind of attention I was being taught for practicing psychotherapy. Sigmund Freud called it "evenly hovering attention."[1] Later Wilfred Bion, also a prominent psychoanalyst, described it as "listening without desire, memory, or understanding."[2] Irv Yalom, existential psychiatrist and preeminent authority on group psychotherapy, was supervising us at Stanford in group psychotherapy. He taught us that, while the group members would be drawn into talking about things that happened somewhere else and some other time, we should pay attention to what was *actually happening in the room, in each moment*, and help the group members pay attention to that also.

As therapists, we're trained in the art of having conversations that help people. We're taught to listen with evenly hovering attention and mindfulness and to perceive freshly what is actually unfolding in that moment. We're also taught to listen to our own inner experiences and to be informed by this experience. We're taught to speak mindfully to help our clients hear us, to speak in such a way that the door of their willingness to participate will not slam shut, or if it does, to wait patiently and lovingly to help it reopen. We're taught that the relationship comes first and that we must be aware of the effect on that relationship of every moment. We're taught that our words should further understanding and learning and that *our own* learning is part of the deal.

It became clear to me when I opened my practice that beyond using these skills myself as I worked with couples, I needed to teach *them* to use these same skills with each other!

The book that you hold in your hands is my attempt to share with you what I've learned from thousands of hours spent with couples as they bravely and persistently made their way toward each other. I've made suggestions and then observed closely what worked and what didn't. These recipes are kitchen tested.

As we go along, I'll share with you my clinical experience as well as research that informs us about relationships. I've given you some interesting things to *read*. I've also given you exercises, or experiments, so that you can *learn by doing*. In my office, couples learn by having conversations, often hard ones, and finding out how to open up to each other and how to use their awareness of that openness to navigate their difficulties. I'm going to guide you through this process with the exercises so that you can see for yourself what works, and what doesn't.

My husband and I joke that we each married the most impossible person ever, necessitating lots of learning! These recipes were developed and tested in that kitchen also.

TURNING PROBLEMS INTO LEARNING

You're probably reading this because you're part of a couple. And while you are reading this, somewhere other couples are flirting and fighting, taking long walks, having hard talks that bring them closer, having hard talks that seem endless and make things worse, becoming angry over small misunderstandings, looking forward to having sex, having sex, wishing they knew how to fall in love again, falling in love again, feeling wrong and wronged, kissing, and feeling contented, disappointed, desperate, and ecstatic.

When the Honeymoon Is Over

When we decide to become a couple, we have in mind love, support, companionship, and the realization of mutually held dreams, such as creating a family or seeing the world together. At some point, though, we inevitably run headlong into unexpected difficulties. We may start to wonder what happened to the person we once loved, the person we once were.

We begin to realize that our partner does not, in fact, meet all our needs. We experience the difficulty of actually functioning as a team in a myriad of situations. While an unusual amount of like-mindedness brought us together, the differences between the two of us in perceptions, preferences, timing, and so on can become daunting, sometimes excruciating.

This other person seems to have a mind that is, in fact, their own. Thinking, deciding, and acting together is much harder than thinking, deciding, and acting alone.

Then there are the ways that intimate connection confronts us, uncomfortably, with aspects of ourselves. Once partnered, we discover that we have given this other person a front-row seat to observe us, including behaviors that we aren't aware of and things we don't like about ourselves.

Finally, everything we do affects our partner and vice versa. This raises new questions about autonomy in the context of relationship. We face the growing understanding that the demands of this relationship are much larger than we imagined; coupling requires more of us than we knew. More time, more energy, more learning. Life has pulled a bit of a bait and switch. We begin to feel that a great deal is at stake; there's no easy exit, and we have no idea how to proceed. The perfect storm—or the perfect conditions for learning.

The Problems Are Not the Problem

At some point, it became clear to me that the problems couples encounter, though difficult and painful, are in fact the gateway to connection and learning. An exciting vision emerged of couples' difficulties as indispensably valuable for health, growth, and expansion. I also began to see this kind of learning as intrinsic to who we are. We are meant to continue to grow as individuals, and we need intimate, committed relationships to do this. Correspondingly, we need to continue to grow individually to form and sustain intimate, committed, satisfying relationships.

Our Western culture makes it hard for couples to experience their difficulties that way. We overvalue uncomplicated romantic bliss, individuality, control, choice, and comfort—all things that an intimate, committed relationship is likely to

disrupt. We undervalue the hard-earned learning that is inseparable from life and love. Often, couples take their difficulties
to mean that they are failing, or even incapable of succeeding,
in their partnership. They worry that perhaps the difficulties
mean they have chosen the wrong person; perhaps *they are* the
wrong person. Conversely, couples may conclude that no one
is succeeding in having a good relationship, that their hopeful expectations are unrealistic, and that they should resign
themselves to the particular brand of misery that is life as a
couple. These conclusions are not true or helpful.

When we change our perspective to see the problems we
encounter in our relationships as doors to our learning and
development as individuals and as a couple, they can lead us to
growth that makes us stronger and more loving.

In mythology and fairy tales, the bearers of gifts or wisdom are often disguised as something or someone unappealing or even dangerous. The protagonist spends a great deal of
time and energy trying to ignore, defeat, or get rid of the troublesome "problem." Along the way, they have many adventures
and finally acquire wisdom or wealth. Just so with relationships: Those things we initially encounter as problems often
lead us to hidden treasure. Turning your problems into learning is the difference between struggling and thriving. Turning
problems into learning is both the hard work and the hidden
treasure.

If you are reading this, it likely means that your relationship is important to you, that you care about it being an alive
and fulfilling part of your life, and that you are taking action in
response to your concerns.

This is the moment of opportunity.

The Four Practices

The life of every couple is full of moments of confusing feelings, thoughts, words, behaviors, motivations, memories, fears, and desires. How can we possibly navigate this complexity? The radically simple answer: by turning all our attention to what is happening in the moment, each moment, as we interact with each other.

Turning our attention to *now* is different from what we usually do. Generally we use our thoughts, constructions, models, and abstractions to steer our lives. Our big brains are constantly busy figuring out what's going on and what to do next. In life with our partners we too often try to understand and act based on what's happened in the past or on theories and ideas about why people feel and act the way they do. When relationships are in trouble, for a moment, or for much longer, couples can get very occupied with thinking. This can get in the way of simply paying attention to what is happening right now, in the moment, as you interact. Both the information we need and the ability to make a positive difference are found in each present moment. This book teaches you to use four essential, interrelated practices to develop and use your present moment awareness: aperture awareness, dialogue, mindfulness, and learning.

- *Aperture awareness* is the ability to sense, in the moment, your own openness and that of your partner.
- *Dialogue* is the ability to use aperture awareness to have conversations that make things better instead of worse.
- *Mindfulness* is the ability to be aware of what is happening inside you and between the two of you in any given moment.
- *Learning* is the ability to direct your own learning and to become learning partners.

Let's take a closer look at these practices so you have a foundational knowledge that will support your learning.

Aperture Awareness

Aperture is the word I use to describe the dynamic, constantly changing openness for connection between people. Everything we want from each other—caring, understanding, fun, and forgiveness—all depend upon openness. Without it, nothing is possible.

Our apertures are highly sensitive and changing all the time in response to internal and external factors. We have the somewhat amazing ability to sense our own apertures and those of others. This ability, *aperture awareness*, allows us to use in-the-moment information to decrease moments of hurting each other and increase connection. Openness, aperture, is the North Star. Attention to openness, aperture awareness, is how we navigate.

In Part One you'll learn to recognize, strengthen, and use aperture awareness. We'll also review the related neuroscience. Aperture awareness makes possible, and is made possible by, the other three practices: mindfulness, dialogue, and learning. You'll hear me emphasize this interrelatedness throughout the book.

Dialogue

Dialogue refers to a particular kind of conversation, one in which the participants are allies, each invested in the other's well-being. Part Two focuses on dialogue as collaborative learning that prioritizes the relationship. This kind of communication is essential to deepening your relationship and learning from conflict. In dialogue, new ideas emerge and understanding expands. You'll learn how to have conversations that are true dialogues, how to distinguish dialogue from other kinds of conversation, how to shift from adversarial conversation to dialogue, and how to deal with some of the most common difficulties couples encounter in their conversations.

Aperture awareness is necessary for skillful dialogue, and dialogue makes aperture awareness and openness possible. Parts One and Two are designed to work as a progression from basic skills and understandings to more complex ones. So, I would suggest you approach these two sections as they are presented.

Mindfulness

Mindfulness, or mindful awareness, is the ability to be aware of your experience—thoughts, perceptions, feelings, motivations, and behaviors—in the present moment, without judgment. Curiosity and neutral awareness lead to greater understanding and the power to make conscious decisions about your behaviors.

Mindfulness, explored in Part Three, is required for, and develops as a result of, aperture awareness and dialogue. As you do the exercises in Parts One and Two, you'll inevitably discover more about what's difficult for you. As you do, you may find it helpful to take a look at Part Three for ideas about how to use mindfulness for these challenges.

Learning

When couples are in difficulty, one of the big questions they have is "Can people really change?" Yes, of course! Change is learning, and our capacity for learning is vast and continues throughout life. Much of adult learning and development happens in relationships, particularly in couples. The better question is: How do we get better at learning and change?

Understanding how to participate skillfully in your own and each other's learning makes change possible. In Part Four we'll explore the conditions for learning and the ways that couples can work together to bring about the changes they want.

If you are feeling discouraged or pessimistic about whether you'll be able to improve your relationship, you might take a look at Part Four to help you understand why your efforts may not have produced the desired results yet and what might work better.

Relationship Spirals

In relationships there are upward spirals and downward spirals. Sometimes relationships are doing well and improving; sometimes they are in trouble, getting worse. And while couples do at times look for books to make a good relationship better, more often they look for help when they are concerned and in a downward spiral. This book is meant for couples in either of these phases. The skills you'll learn to turn a downward spiral into an upward spiral will also make a good relationship better.

Why Do Relationships Spiral?

Almost any action or interaction has in it some ambiguity, or room for interpretation. We are constantly filling in the blanks—speculating on the meanings and motivations of what our partner said or did. We even fill in the blanks concerning the actual words spoken or actions taken. Our auditory and visual perceptions involve a process of filling in the blanks of imperfectly perceived stimuli. No wonder couples so often don't even agree about what was actually said or done![3]

In an upward spiral, we fill in the blanks with positive assumptions and interpretations—we give the benefit of the doubt. So, when things are good, they tend to get better. In a downward spiral, we fill in with negative assumptions—we assume the worst. When things are not so good, they tend to get worse. For example, your partner schedules a business meeting Saturday at the time of your daughter's soccer game. In an upward cycle you might not like it, but you will either assume that they did this for good reasons, keeping the needs of the family in mind, or realize you don't know what they had in mind and ask in an open, curious way.

If, on the other hand, you're in a downward spiral, you may see this as the next in a series of screwups or imagine it means they're not interested in the soccer game, your daughter, or even the family. And you likely will not check this out by asking them. Or, if you do, you'll ask in a way that feels accusatory and makes them defensive.

In a downward spiral, lack of trust leads to negative assumptions and the next damaging interaction that further diminishes trust. Susan Johnson, clinical psychologist and developer of Emotionally Focused Therapy (EFT), described it as "a circular loop of hurt and despair."[4]

In an upward spiral, positive assumptions lead to exchanges that further build trust. In an upward spiral, you'll still have misunderstandings and disagreements, but the overall experience of the relationship is positive. In a downward spiral, your relationship has become a source of more pain than pleasure.

HOW DO YOU RECOGNIZE A
DOWNWARD SPIRAL?

Perhaps as soon as I said "downward spiral," you recognized your experience. Couples in a downward spiral may describe themselves as discouraged, sad, hopeless, or at the end of their rope. Below are several behaviors characteristic of a downward spiral:

- Engaging with each other at the wrong times, in the wrong ways
- Disengaging at the wrong times, in the wrong ways
- Keeping score
- Focusing on your partner's mistakes
- Negative expectations
- Defensiveness
- Decreased trust
- Feeling despair

Spirals and Getting Discouraged

In a downward spiral, it's easy to get discouraged. We feel like our efforts to make things better aren't working. Lacking understanding about how change happens in relationships, we often try the wrong experiments, misinterpret the results, or both. When things get hard, we do what we know how to do to try to remedy the situation. Sometimes it works. But when it doesn't, we often keep trying the same thing—thinking maybe we just need to do it *better or louder.* We may end up exhausting ourselves and even making things worse.

Relationships act like physical objects in motion: They tend to continue in the direction they're going. To get out of a downward spiral, you first have to reverse the direction of the spiral—by far the hardest part. Sometimes couples become overly discouraged, thinking that the work of making things better, which can feel very hard initially, will always be this hard. Fortunately, this is not true. Once you reverse the spiral, your work gets easier and the benefits larger.

If you've ever had to get a stuck car out of the mud, you know that moving it the first few inches to get the tires out of the deep rut they've carved is the hardest part. It can take a lot of time and patience to gather materials, lay a solid surface in front of the tires, adjust everything, and then give just the right push to get the initial movement. But once there's traction, the car rolls forward with much less effort. Reversing a downward spiral is a little like that.

For reversing the spiral, as in unsticking a mud-mired car, you need to know what kinds of efforts to make and that an initial well-placed and energetic effort may succeed in getting your relationship moving up instead of down.

Note: In this book I am not going to talk directly about sex. Some of you are probably relieved to hear this, others disappointed. Given how important sex is in many couples' relationships, I have included some thoughts about this choice in appendix A (page 267).

LEARNING BY READING AND LEARNING BY DOING

This book contains ideas from psychotherapy, mindfulness,

and neuroscience and is also a guided training in the practices—aperture awareness, dialogue, mindfulness, and learning—that will help you transform your relationship.

Reading

Research—clinical, behavioral, and neuroscientific—expands our understanding of what goes on inside us and between us. In this book we'll look at, for example, how our information processing influences our interactions, how early parent-child interactions affect what happens in our adult relationships, what behaviors characterize relationships that last, how our brains affect our relationships, and how our relationships shape our brains.

Sometimes scientific insights help us experience our emotions and behaviors with more compassion and curiosity and understand what doesn't work and what might work better. The discovery of neuroplasticity—our brain's capacity to adapt—tells us that we can grow and change over the course of a lifetime. We're learning how relationships can support those very changes.

As you read, you'll encounter some ideas that are familiar or quickly fit with what you already know. You'll also find concepts that either don't make sense to you or seem contradictory to what you know. When you come across ideas that don't fit, I encourage you to sit with the old and the new, side by side. Don't discard either right away. Instead, try to understand how they might both be true, related, and helpful despite their seeming contradictions. In Part Two, you'll learn how this skill—simultaneously holding two uncomfortably different realities—is essential to dialogue.

Doing

Learning by doing is the heart of this book. Eminent psychiatrist Harry Stack Sullivan said, "It is easier to act yourself into a new way of feeling than to feel yourself into a new way of acting."[5] The shortcut to insight and change is often action. Throughout the book, information will be followed by exercises—new ways of interacting.

Many traditional therapies focus on the past as a source of insight and change. While this can be helpful, there are two problems with this approach: (1) Insight does not always lead to change, and (2) gaining insight by exploring one's past can take a very long time, usually longer than a couple in trouble can afford to spend.

The new behaviors in the exercises will help you to connect and have better conversations—sometimes the first time you try them. As you repeat them, the positive effects will increase.

The exercises will also help increase your awareness. The habitual, reactive behaviors that cause problems in relationships are largely unconscious. When we inhibit these reactions, we become more aware of thoughts, feelings, and behaviors that are problematic. Your expanded awareness is even more powerful than the behaviors themselves in improving your relationship.

As you do the exercises, everything you experience is part of your learning. Allow yourself to experiment without specific ideas of what success looks like. Let yourself be surprised.

Some of the exercises may feel artificial. You may feel awkward or experience a sense of "This is not me." This is entirely normal. Remember, these are experiments. Like practicing scales to learn piano, these exercises are meant to help you focus on a specific aspect of your interactions. Try them on. You can figure out later how, or if, they fit your authentic self. If you feel uncomfortable, try to observe your experience with nonjudgmental curiosity. Even awkwardness can help you to be mindful. Any outcome, including not being able to do a particular exercise, is useful if you can pay attention to what was difficult for you.

Be patient with yourself and your partner. Anything you learn from an exercise, even if it is only to notice that the exercise frustrates you, can be valuable. Some exercises will seem easy, others hard. Even this provides information about what you're already skilled at and what challenges you.

Most of the exercises are conversations. Conversations have two aspects: what you talk about (content) and how you talk (process). For most exercises you choose the content. The exercises then are experiments with *how* you talk about your topic. Though it can seem like *what* you're talking about is causing the difficulties, in fact it is *how* you talk to each other that usually makes all the difference!

You'll notice right away that during the exercises, you do not finish the conversation, solve the problem, or even get to fully express yourself. This may feel frustrating. We are goal oriented and expect an outcome, even in our intimate conversations. This frustration is an opportunity in itself. The purpose of the exercises is not to resolve or come to closure. You are learning to de-emphasize resolution and pay attention to how the conversation is affecting you and your partner.

Repeat the exercises until the new behaviors and awareness become natural, automatic. When an exercise seems particularly helpful, you can also increase the length of time. Practice until it's no longer an exercise but part of how you talk to each other.

For all exercises, you will need a comfortable, private place to talk, two notebooks, two pens or pencils, and a timer. For most exercises, there will be a specified length of time to talk, after which you will need ten to twenty minutes for reflection, writing, and discussion. As with the exercises themselves, the ease and value of the writing and reflection will increase as you go. This is an aspect of learning how to learn. Always process with yourself before discussing with your partner.

The final step, a discussion, is a brief exchange of whatever each of you wants to say. Use it as a time to discuss your learning; don't go back into the content of your conversation. There is no right or wrong, better or worse, to what you learned. Write down any ideas that emerge.

Most importantly, have fun. You will be working together on things that are difficult and important. Especially at the beginning, be gentle and kind with yourself, and if the exercise is asking too much, scale it down. This should be somewhat hard, but not *too* hard. Make efforts that are sustainable and enlivening. Find the balance of seriousness and playfulness.

Bon voyage!

A Note to Therapists

This book is for couples *and* for therapists. You will find here a mindfulness-based approach that is a synthesis of my training as a psychiatrist, my experiences with Buddhism and meditation, and the neuroscience of relationships. If you are new to couples work, I hope this book will help you chart a course through the potentially confusing complexity of working with couples. If you're an experienced couples therapist, the ideas may enhance your current models and skills. This is not a model to replace others but a way to add simplicity and clarity to your work.

In my conversations with therapists, I find that some love to work with couples and others don't. Those who don't say they find working with couples too complicated and too difficult. They are describing the experience couples themselves are having. Using in-the-moment awareness of openness, aperture awareness, as the primary focus makes steering the ship easier, more accurate, and more enjoyable—for you and for your couples.

At some point in teaching colleagues about aperture, I realized that our own aperture awareness is the foundation for *all* our work. Underneath all our models, techniques, procedures, and words—when we are most effective—we are being guided by our awareness of openness, our own and our clients'. This aspect of our work is often in the background, largely unconscious. I've given it a name, aperture awareness, and put it in the foreground. And I've taught couples to use it as the central focus of their attention as they steer through the complex challenges of relationship. By understanding more about the centrality of openness, we may be able to use this power even more effectively.

There are many ways you can use this book. You might recommend it as a resource for your couples. You might read it yourself and let the ideas and practices inform what you do. You might use it as a source of exercises for sessions and homework or as a step-by-step guide that you and your clients follow together. My wish is that this book makes your work with couples more effective and more fun.

PART ONE

Aperture and Aperture Awareness

There are two pillars of happiness. . . . One is love. The other is finding a way of coping with life that does not push love away.

—George Vaillant[1]

CHAPTER 1

What Is Aperture?

Every encounter between living things requires a basic decision: open or close? The bluebird outside my window hops over to the bush with the bright red berries. Faster than I can write this sentence, he opens his mouth and grabs the berry—a split-second decision to open. A moment later, he spies my cat creeping around the yard and takes off. Where contact with the cat is concerned, he is closed.

Aperture is the word I use to describe the dynamic, constantly changing openness for connection between people. Aperture is the central focus of this book because it is the foundation for all the skills, awareness, and understanding that make relationships work. Aperture is the North Star for finding your way through the confusing complexity that is life as a couple. In this chapter we begin the exploration of what aperture is and why it's so important.

Apertures regulate countless processes within living things as well as connections between living things. Cellular membranes have ionic channels, microscopic apertures, that open and close to regulate the level of salt in the cell. The irises in our eyes (models for the photographic aperture) are continuously adjusting our pupils to let in the right amount of light for our vision. Anyone who has had the unique pleasure of feeding a toddler knows the train game, a maneuver for coaxing the child's mouth—aperture—to open for the next spoonful. And then there are our emotional apertures, the focus of this book.

Our emotional aperture is our willingness or unwillingness to receive each other, to welcome communication, contact, and shared experience. Think about common phrases we use like "She just wasn't open to my ideas," "You had me at hello," or "I'm just not buying it." All of these refer to some basic sense of being open or closed. "We regulate empathy by opening or closing a door, depending on who we identify with and feel close to. We open the door wide for friends and relatives, and for animals that we love, but we close it for enemies and for animals we don't care about," wrote primatologist Frans de Waal in *Mama's Last Hug*.[1] The "door" he is talking about is aperture.

When it comes to human beings, the ramifications and complexity of opening and closing are infinite. We may initially make a decision that's sort of simple, like the bluebird with the berry: "I like the way you look, and I like the way you taste." Open. But then contact and connection can trigger our survival system, the responses we know as fight-flight-freeze.

Unlike the bluebird fleeing the cat, our sense of unsafety rarely involves fear of being eaten. Yet the feeling and the instantaneous closing response are very much the same. The trigger can be as subtle as a change in tone of voice or as large as the discovery of an affair. And whereas the bluebird is always open to the red berry and always closed to the cat, our aperture to our partner is constantly in motion, shifting and flickering between open and closed.

"It is a pleasure to be hidden, and a disaster not to be found," wrote D. W. Winnicott, an English pediatrician and psychoanalyst who played a major role in our understanding of how the self develops.[2] To expand a little on Winnicott's idea, sometimes it's wise to be hidden, other times unwise. To be wide-open all the time exposes us to more of life's emotional pain than we can handle. Sometimes we really are in danger emotionally and need a way to shut down, limiting our exposure to insults, betrayals, or abandonments. Sometimes we want to be hidden. Then again, sometimes we are offered wonderful experiences of love and beauty. If we are closed, we miss out. Sometimes we want to be found.

Life in relationships is about enjoying the pleasure of being known and contacted, while minimizing the possibility of injury. Ideally, we have flexible and responsive apertures that open when love and connection are possible and close when harm seems more likely. Happiness and safety in couples depends on changing apertures regulating a delicate balance of separate and together, hidden and found, closed and open.

OPEN TO CONNECTION

People choose to be in a couple in order to experience the joys of connection, whether for safety, companionship, sex, or some combination. We want and need connection, and we're well designed for it, with brains that jump-start the process by providing good feelings when connections are made.

When we talk about having chemistry with someone, it's not just a metaphor. Certain connections set off the delivery of love potions, of dopamine and oxytocin. Dopamine, one of the neurochemicals in our brain that causes us to feel good, is released in response to all kinds of connections—from the tiny neuronal links that form when we learn something new to the passions that flame between new lovers. When it's released, we feel good and want more. (This dopamine reward fuels healthy habits like learning and exercise as well as potentially unhealthy ones, like nicotine and alcohol.) Oxytocin, which encourages empathy and bonding, is released after sex and during childbirth and nursing, nudging us, neurochemically, toward long-lasting relationships.[3]

Connection with others is essential, not just for the survival of the species but also for our individual health. Many of our physiological systems, including cardiovascular, hormonal, digestive, and immunological systems, are regulated, in part, by our contact with each other.[4] One study found that in patients recovering from heart attacks, social isolation tripled the death rate. Physician Dean Ornish, surveying the medical literature on the relationship between isolation and mortality, concluded that social isolation dramatically increased premature mortality from all causes.[5]

PHYSICAL CONTACT IS ESSENTIAL TO SURVIVAL

In a famous study from the 1940s, psychoanalyst René Spitz reported on orphaned infants who were being fed, clothed, and cared for physically but, in deference to the recent discovery of germs as the cause of illness, were not handled, played with, or held. Spitz found that these babies became withdrawn and sickly and were, in fact, more vulnerable to the very infections their isolation was meant to protect them from.[6] This was one of the first pieces of definitive evidence for something many cultures had known all along: human beings need physical contact with each other in order to survive.

"Interdependence is and ought to be as much the ideal of man as self-sufficiency. Man is a social being," wrote Mohandas/Mahatma Gandhi.[7] Western culture emphasizes self-sufficiency and tacitly promotes the idea of human beings as closed systems. In fact, we are open systems, in constant contact and interaction with other beings, especially other humans. Psychologist Louis Cozolino talks about the "social synapse," meaning that we are connected neurologically to each other, just as the neurons in our individual brains are linked to each other through synapses. Cozolino says, "Neither the individual neuron, nor the individual human exists in nature."[8] Or as playwright Tony Kushner put it, "The smallest indivisible human unit is two."[9]

In Edward Tronick's famous still-face experiment in the 1970s, researchers observed infants' reactions when their mothers stopped interacting with them and instead kept their faces entirely blank. After only three minutes of trying in vain to elicit a response, the infants would give up, withdraw, and turn away from the mothers with an expression of distress. From the beginning of life, we count on other people, not only for the essentials of biological survival but for emotional, psychological connection.[10]

In another study, researchers used fMRI technology to visualize brain changes related to stress. When women were shown disturbing images, their brains showed a clear increase in stress, but stress levels were much lower in those who were allowed to hold their partner's hand during the experiment. Furthermore, the better the women reported feeling about their relationships, the greater the soothing effect![11]

"Love is the best survival mechanism there is," wrote Susan Johnson, developer of Emotionally Focused Therapy. "This longing for emotional connection with those nearest to us is *the* emotional priority, overshadowing even the drive for food or sex. The drama of love is all about this hunger for safe emotional connection."[12]

So, if connection feels so good, and if it's so vital for our well-being, why is it so hard?

CLOSED TO CONNECTION

Our apertures close when we feel we're losing our partner or ourselves. A part of the brain known as the amygdala is always processing our experience for any sign of danger. This part makes sure we are not going to get eaten, or experience the emotional equivalent of that, when a situation sours. When a potential threat is detected, the amygdala responds with lightning speed. The *danger! danger!* signal is activated, sending various body systems into a state of tension.[13] We are ready for fighting, fleeing, or freezing—the opposite of emotional openness.

As part of a couple, you know how powerfully this survival response can be triggered. You know how disorienting it is to feel frightened or angry in the presence of someone you love, to feel yourself close off to them. Intimacy, it turns out, can feel dangerous. You are extremely vulnerable to this person, by nature of your interdependence, and so your fears of disapproval, rejection, and abandonment are amplified. The same need for connection that motivates us to be open to each other becomes the impetus to close when we fear the loss of that connection. In fact, the strongest trigger for our own aperture to close is the sense that our partner's has closed.

The other trigger for the danger response and aperture closure is when we feel that our autonomy is threatened. In life as a couple, it can feel like our individual integrity is at odds with maintaining the connection. We fear that we'll lose ourselves. This fear is often what lies behind a preoccupation with being right or a dogged insistence on fairness. In fact, connection and autonomy are complementary. The success of a couple's ongoing integration process depends on both.

APERTURE AWARENESS AND RESONANCE

Our emotional apertures, like most of our physiological apertures, open and close without our awareness or conscious control. Yet, unlike most of our other apertures, we have the ability to become aware of our emotional aperture. This is analogous to breathing; we can abandon it to automatic functioning or engage to observe and participate. With aperture awareness, we become capable of more openness to increase connection and learning. Aperture awareness also makes it possible to minimize damage when apertures are closing.

We can sense not only our own apertures but those of other people—aperture resonance. Our brains evolved to monitor both our internal states and the internal states of others.[14] Because of this, we are constantly reacting to our sense of the other person's openness, but usually without awareness. With aperture awareness you become consciously aware of both your own aperture and that of your partner. (For a description of the neurology of aperture awareness, take a look at the box on page 34, "Aperture and the Limbic System.")

Aperture awareness is a felt sensation. Our brains process vast amounts of information, more than we can possibly

capture in thoughts or words. Just as we do not see by consciously thinking about the information our eyes absorb, we
do not become aware of aperture through thought and analysis. Rather, we learn to feel it, to become aware of it and then
to pay careful attention. Simply asking yourself, "Do I feel
open or closed right now?" directs your attention to this felt
experience.

An open aperture feels like safety, relaxation, trust, op-
timism. A closed aperture feels like danger, wariness, pessimism, anxiety, unease. Some people register these physically.
Looseness, softness, and warmth often signal an open aperture. Tightness, hardness, or coldness, especially in your chest
or belly, often coincide with a closed aperture.

For some of you, aperture awareness is available easily,
even though you've never heard the term before. For others,
it may come more slowly. If all of this seems a bit vague, don't
worry. The following exercises will help you tune in to your
aperture and build that awareness over time. And, like other
senses, aperture awareness becomes stronger as we learn how
to use it.

Exercise: Preparing Your Topics

In this exercise, you'll develop a list of potential topics to work
with throughout this book. You will want to keep this list of
topics handy. You may want to think of it this way: What are
some of the topics that recur in your relationship and that, if
you could have a really good talk about them, might enhance
your relationship?

1. Each of you makes a list of topics that you want or
    need to discuss with your partner.

2. Then, on the left side of the page, assign a rating 1, 2, or 3 for each topic by the level of *difficulty* with 1 = very easy; 2 = moderately hard; 3 = very hard. On the right, assign a number for the level of *importance* of this topic: 1 = mildly important; 2 = medium importance; 3 = very important.

Example:
Partner A

Difficulty		**Importance**
3	finances	3
3	sex	2
2	whether or not to move	1
1	household chores	1

Partner B

Difficulty		**Importance**
1	his family	2
2	the kid's school	3
3	sex	3
1	finances	2

3. Go over your lists together. There are probably some items that appear on both lists, but you may find some surprises.
4. Now choose one topic to use for the first few exercises. The topic should be one that is important to each of you (though it needn't be one that you each put on your list) and likely to be moderately challenging but not overwhelming. I suggest that you stick with the same topic for a few exercises. When you feel you've exhausted the possibilities of your topic, return to your lists and choose another.

You may want to repeat this exercise at certain points to discover other topics.

Exercise: Aperture Awareness

In this exercise, while having a twenty-minute conversation about one of your topics, you are going to begin practicing aperture awareness. (Note: For all exercises allow at least an additional ten minutes for *Reflect and write* and *Discuss*.) In this exercise you will simply use the general question, *Open or closed?* about your own aperture and your sense of your partner's aperture to see what you can detect. In the subsequent two exercises, you'll practice with awareness of some of the specific elements of aperture. Practice several times with these three exercises before moving on to the rest of the chapter, and return to them intermittently to strengthen aperture awareness as you add other skills. Patience and practice will help you solidify this central skill.

1. Select a mildly or moderately difficult topic from your list. You will talk for about twenty minutes.
2. Check in and record your apertures before you begin, using a 1–10 scale (1 = entirely closed; 10 = entirely open). Openness is a continuum. Assign a number to your apertures rather than simply describing them as open or closed. This will help you strengthen aperture awareness.
3. Set the timer for five minutes and begin your conversation. When the timer goes off, pause the conversation and note your own aperture and your sense of your partner's aperture. Then check in with each other about your apertures and

record your partner's sense of their own aperture
and of yours.

4. Set your timer for another five minutes and pro-
    ceed as before through four more check-ins. (Start
    the five minutes after each of you has finished
    recording your aperture notes so that you have
    time to record without feeling rushed before the
    next five-minute piece of conversation begins.)
    Your record should look something like this:

Date _____ Exercise _____

Check-In #1 (before beginning)

Your sense of your aperture _____
Your sense of your partner's aperture _____
Your partner's sense of their aperture _____
Your partner's sense of your aperture _____
And so on, through five check-ins.

5. Though you may be tempted to continue the con-
    versation, stop when you finish the fifth check-in.
    Remember, this is an experiment, not a full
    conversation.

6. *Reflect and write*, independently, considering the
    following questions:

- How challenging was this exercise?
- How closely did your sense of the apertures
  match your partner's?
- If they did not match very well, how are you feel-
  ing about and thinking about those differences?
- Do the differences make you curious?
  Uncomfortable? Other reactions?

- What else did you notice?
- What did you learn?

7. *Discuss*: Spend a few minutes talking about your experiences and what you learned. Remember that the goal of the exercise and the discussion is to learn. Avoid being critical, either of yourself or your partner. Stay curious.
8. Close with appreciations for yourself and your partner for this experiment. Doing this work requires effort, risk-taking, and time. Help each other value that.

APERTURE AND THE LIMBIC SYSTEM

Aperture is the felt experience of our brains' lightning-speed processing of a thick stream of information related to our connections with others and the likelihood of danger or satisfaction. Or to put it in Winnicott's terms: Is it a good moment to be hidden or to be found?

In a part of the brain known as the limbic system, massive amounts of information are processed. (A data stream with resolution fine enough to catch the subtleties of facial expression requires about four hundred kilobits per second![15]) We are capable of, among other astonishing feats, sensing, regulating, and changing each other's internal states. This is sometimes referred to as limbic *resonance, regulation,* and *revision*.[16] These abilities are the basis of empathy as well as the sadness we can feel when empathy fails. They are at the heart of the experiences we think of as uniquely human, though we share some of these abilities and connections with other mammals as well.

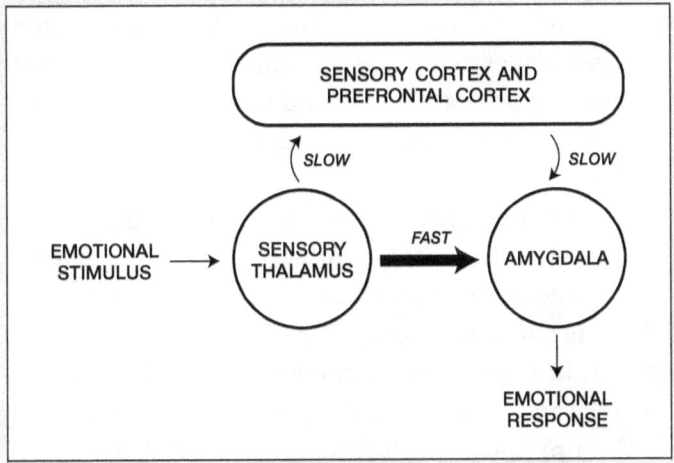

Figure 1: Limbic Processing: Fast and Slow[17]

Information travels through the limbic system in two pathways, one designed for speed and the other for accuracy and complexity. For both pathways, sensory information first enters through the thalamus. In the fast system, it then travels to the amygdala, a powerful area for processing information about safety and other input to which evolution has given top priority. Interestingly, this top priority list includes facial expressions.[18] (Somewhere in our progress toward human complexity, the brain decided that facial expressions were top priority to our survival and well-being.)

The amygdala, always erring on the side of caution, instantly signals the hypothalamus of the possible need for an emergency reaction of fight-flight-freeze. The hypothalamus then prepares the body, dosing it with adrenaline and cortisol, for the rapid mobilization of energy to get the cardiovascular system geared up. This fast system is responsible for the times when we notice our heart racing and our stomach tightening even before we have any idea of what we are reacting to.

Meanwhile, the same sensory signal is making its way through the second pathway from the thalamus to the neocortex, that most recently evolved surface of the brain, where complex patterns are stitched together. In the neocortex, the information is analyzed for relevance and accuracy. This analysis is fed back to the amygdala, which sends a modified signal to the hypothalamus, based on this new and more extensive evaluation. The hypothalamus then modifies its directions to the body. The second pathway involves many more neuronal connections than the first, which accounts for it taking 0.25 seconds longer and for its ability to render more accurate and complex analyses.

It goes something like this: There is a sinuous shape on the ground. Before you know consciously that your eyes sent a signal, your amygdala has fired the red alert "Possible snake—danger!" and your body is jolted into action. Less than a second later, the second signal from the cortex arrives both in the amygdala and in your conscious awareness: "No, not a snake, only a garden hose." It will now take a few minutes for the cortisol and adrenaline boost to clear your system and your body to return to a resting state.

In interactions with our partner, this process of

limbic sensing and response is going on all the time as we unconsciously evaluate signals including our partner's facial expressions and voice tones. There is a constantly fluctuating balance of danger and safety signals, which is the felt experience of aperture being closed (danger) or open (safety).[19]

Because of limbic resonance, partners' apertures are very responsive to each other. This means that when one of you starts to close, the other is likely to follow—I call this *aperture resonance*. When we are unaware that our own aperture is closing, we can be blindsided by our partner's resonant closing and becoming unavailable. Here's an example of what that might look like:

Blair: I'd like to get a run in today. (Aperture 10)
Davis: Great, me too. How about before dinner? (10)
Blair: Actually, I need to go check on my mom before dinner, so I was thinking about going now. (10)
Davis: Check on your mom? Again? (5)
Blair: Of course, you know I need to do that, right? (5)
Davis: Every day?! (4)
Blair: [Big sigh.] Do you have to control every minute of my time? I'm going running now. Come or don't come, I don't care! (2)

As Davis sees it, Blair got testy for no reason. Davis was simply asking for information. Davis feels Blair's mother is intruding on time that used to be for the two of them. His aperture started to close when Blair mentioned going to see her; his voice tightened and Blair started closing in response.

Neither of them was consciously aware, yet as Davis's aperture closes, Blair's does too. Their apertures are following each other downward until Blair loses his temper, speaks from a very closed aperture, and essentially gives Davis a verbal shove: "Come or don't come, I don't care!"

With more aperture awareness, the exchange might have gone differently:

Blair: I'd like to get a run in today. (10)

Davis: Great, me too. How about before dinner? (10)

Blair: Actually, I need to check on my mom before dinner, so I was thinking about going now. (10)

Davis: [Notices himself tighten, hears internally his first response: "Check on your mom again?!" and notes that his aperture has closed. He pauses to process and partially reopen, then speaks.] Oh, I guess I forgot that you might need to do that today. (5)

Blair: [Feels his aperture close a bit. Remembers that they have been having tension about his mom. Decides this is not the time to discuss that and focuses on holding his own aperture open.] Yeah, I really do. Maybe I could do that a bit earlier and we could get in a run after that and before dinner? (8)

Davis: [Hearing Blair's attempt to stay open, his aperture opens a bit more.] Sure, that would be great. (7)

Blair: Cool, so let's run around six, maybe go to the reservoir? (8)

Davis: Sounds good. (8)

The best way to help your partner keep an open aperture is to stay aware of your own and learn how to keep it open.

We will talk more in Part Two about collaborating to keep apertures open, but here is a pair of exercises to begin raising awareness about the elements of your own and your partner's apertures.

Exercise: Sensing the Elements of Your Aperture

Aperture awareness is the result of an enormous capacity in our brains to gather huge streams of data and synthesize them into recognizable experiences. The previous exercise focused on recognition of the felt sense of aperture as a whole experience—a composite of the millions of stimuli your nervous system is processing all the time.

It can be helpful to break this awareness down into its parts to see how your brilliant limbic system is doing its work. This deconstructed approach will enable you to focus your attention on one or two familiar feelings that are actually components of your aperture.

1. This exercise has a similar structure to Aperture Awareness (page 32). Using your selected topic, you will talk for about twenty minutes.
2. Set the timer to cue you every five minutes. Each time it goes off, pause the conversation and take the following inventory of your experience, using a 1–10 scale to indicate how true the statement is: 1 = not at all; 10 = very. (For example, for the first statement, 10 indicates you're entirely at ease; 1 that you are feeling tense. For the second statement, 10 is delighted to be having this conversation; 1 is miserable, and so on.) As before, start with an initial check-in with yourself:

Check-In #1 (before beginning)

I feel relaxed _____

(If you instead feel tense, try to notice where this tension is and what it feels like. Can you feel your jaw clench, your chest tighten, your muscles tense? Make note of those observations here.)

I feel happy to be having this conversation _____

I feel curious about what my partner is saying _____

I feel patient _____

I feel safe, emotionally _____

I feel listened to _____

I feel that my partner is interested in
   understanding me _____

3. Continue this way for five check-ins.
4. *Reflect and write* separately on your experience of this exercise. Sometimes the most important learning is noticing what questions arose as you did the exercise. Be sure to record your questions.
5. *Discuss.*

Exercise: Sensing the Elements of Your Partner's Aperture

1. This exercise has a similar structure to Aperture Awareness (page 32). Using your topic, you will talk for about twenty minutes.
2. Set the timer to cue you every five minutes. Each time it goes off, pause the conversation and take the following inventory for what you *sense* your partner's experience is on the scale of 1–10:

Check-In #1 (before beginning)

My partner feels relaxed _____
       (Make note here of any signs you see of their level of
relaxation, as you did for yourself in the previous exercise.)
My partner feels happy to be having
       this conversation _____
My partner feels curious about what I am saying _____
My partner feels patient _____
My partner feels safe, emotionally _____
My partner feels listened to _____
My partner feels that I am interested
       in understanding them _____

3. Continue this way for five check-ins.
4. *Reflect and write* separately on your experience,
   recording any questions that come up.
5. *Discuss.*

EYE CONTACT AND APERTURE

"There is a road from the eye to the heart that does not go
through the intellect," wrote philosopher G. K. Chesterton.[20]
Eye contact has a powerful impact on our conversations and our
apertures. Eye contact intensifies connection and emotional
experience. In neurological terms, face-to-face contact activates
the sympathetic nervous system, increases brain activity, and
increases norepinephrine, endorphins, and dopamine—all of
which promote brain growth and add to feelings of pleasure.
Face-to-face contact opens us up to each other and allows connections to flourish. That intense mutual gaze between infants
and their caretakers is actually developing their brains.[21]
       We unconsciously interpret the quality of eye contact all

the time in our interactions. Researchers have studied many facets of this phenomenon. If people are sitting close together, for example, they rely less on direct eye contact, perhaps because the physical closeness supplements the intimacy.[22] We watch the eyes of someone listening to us, and we're offended if they look away too often. When we're the listener, we find it particularly disturbing if a speaker averts their gaze while trying to be persuasive. Most people take this as a sign that the speaker is untrustworthy.[23]

Varying eye contact is an important way to modulate your emotional experience and apertures. Sometimes you may want to look away to keep yourself from reacting too intensely to what your partner is saying. At other times you may want to intensify eye contact to emphasize your connection, provide support, or ensure you're being heard. This comes more naturally to some people than others. Some couples use very little eye contact, either because of their own relationship histories or because of difficulties that have developed between them. Increasing your awareness of eye contact can increase aperture awareness and openness.

EYE CONTACT RESEARCH

- We engage in more eye contact if we like each other and if we're cooperating instead of competing.
- Eye contact signals that channels of communication are open.
- We tend to look away when we first start speaking to focus on our thoughts, then look toward our audience near the end of our speech to gather information about how the listener is responding.

- Eye contact can be reinforcing to the verbal behavior of another person.
- Too much eye contact can cause anxiety and may lead to avoidant behaviors.
- Too little eye contact can cause a person to feel deprived of the ability to affiliate.
- Physical proximity produces less eye contact.[24]

Exercise: Eye Contact

For this exercise, your conversation will be divided into three segments, with brief note-taking in between. Allow twenty-five minutes. Prepare by choosing a topic.

1. Set the timer for five minutes and talk about your topic without looking at each other at all. Then pause for a minute or two to each make your own notes:

- How comfortable or uncomfortable was this?
- How did lack of eye contact affect your ability to sense your own aperture?
- How did lack of eye contact affect your ability to sense your partner's aperture?
- Other observations?

2. Set the timer for another five minutes, but this time, face each other and make continuous eye contact. Again, pause to take notes:

- How comfortable or uncomfortable was this?
- How did eye contact affect your ability to sense your own aperture?
- How did eye contact affect your ability to sense your partner's aperture?
- Other observations?

3. For the final ten minutes, you can use eye contact however you like. Pay close attention to what choices you and your partner make, and how they affect aperture and connection. Then pause to make notes:

- How comfortable or uncomfortable was this?
- What did you notice about how you decided to look at or away from your partner?
- Other observations?

4. *Discuss.*

FULL-BODY CONVERSATION

Turning toward your partner allows you to take in essential visual information about how they are doing; it also communicates your interest and attention in a way that can help keep your partner's aperture open.

Your whole body has a face. The front side is the open, vulnerable side; the back is the more protected, armored side. Turning your back on someone is a powerful way of protecting yourself and signaling that you are closed. It is likely to cause the other person to close and become more self-protective.

Turning your front side to another signals readiness for contact and vulnerability, and invites the same in your partner.

This can feel risky, though, especially for a couple in a downward spiral.

In therapy, I often watch couples try to have a conversation without facing each other. They don't completely turn their backs; they just sit shoulder to shoulder, eyes forward. When I suggest they face each other, their first response is often to keep their bodies in the same position and merely swivel their heads toward the other. This doesn't do much to open apertures or invite dialogue. When they offer the face of their whole bodies to each other, their ability to listen, speak, and connect often increases instantly.

For instance, Marge and Tom are in my office having a difficult conversation. As they begin to talk they're sitting on my sofa, each facing forward, toward me, each with their arms crossed. When I ask them to turn toward each other, Tom rotates his body toward Marge ever so slightly; Marge rotates her head only. I'm guessing their apertures are 4 at best.

They are using these postures protectively. Feeling unsafe, they are hiding. But they're also risking, as Winnicott says, the disaster of not being found. So, I acknowledge their vulnerability and insist that they turn to face each other with their whole bodies. When they do, each of them relaxes a bit, shoulders drop, arms uncross, and words and voice tones soften. They begin, tentatively, to make eye contact.

Over the next ten minutes, their apertures move steadily upward. This is a virtuous cycle of aperture resonance. As Tom's aperture opens a bit (maybe from 4 to 4.5), Marge, facing him directly, is able to perceive the change and her aperture moves in response. She's feeling more connected and appreciating his vulnerability. When Tom senses this, he feels reassured and his aperture opens further, and so on. Every turn toward your partner, however slight, makes room for opening.

FULL-BODY-FACING CONTACT

- Turning toward the other person and having an open body posture garners a more positive attitude.
- Open posture conveys accessibility to the other person.
- Leaning forward indicates positive interest.
- Leaning backward or turning away indicates a negative attitude.
- As physical distance decreases, body orientation becomes less direct to compensate.[25]

Exercise: Full-Body Conversation

For this conversation, you will experiment with three different body positions, taking time after each for a few notes.

1. Prepare by choosing a topic and allow twenty-five minutes for your conversation.
2. Sit side by side, facing forward, and set a timer to talk for five minutes. Then pause to separately reflect and write on the following:

- How comfortable or uncomfortable was this?
- How did this position affect your ability to sense your own aperture?
- How did this position affect your ability to sense your partner's aperture?
- What was your aperture during this time?
- Other observations?

3. Sit side by side, looking at each other by turning your heads only, and talk for five minutes.

   • How comfortable or uncomfortable was this?
   • How did this position affect your ability to sense your own aperture?
   • How did this position affect your ability to sense your partner's aperture?
   • What was your aperture during this time?
   • Other observations?

4. Turn so that your whole bodies are facing each other and set a timer for ten minutes. For this part, you do not need to maintain eye contact the whole time; rather notice, as you did in the final ten minutes of the Eye Contact exercise, how you use eye contact and how you experience it from your partner.

5. *Reflect and write:*

   • How comfortable or uncomfortable was this?
   • How did this position affect your ability to sense your own aperture?
   • How did this position affect your ability to sense your partner's aperture?
   • What did you notice about how you used eye contact?
   • What did you notice about how your partner used eye contact?
   • What was your aperture during this time?
   • Other observations?

6. *Discuss.*

CHAPTER 2

Arriving in the Present Moment

The next time you make yourself a warm drink, bring your mind to the present moment. As you open the cabinet to choose a cup, notice the variety of shapes and colors. You may have preferences; notice these reactions. As you reach for the one you'll use, notice the feel of the handle and the weight of the cup in your hand. Hear the sound as you place the cup on the counter. Notice how you decide what you'll have. Do you want the comforting familiarity of what you usually have, or perhaps an adventure with a new choice? Then, can you feel the subtle shift in your body posture and balance as you lift the pot of hot water? See if you can stay fully attentive until the water is poured, your drink is made, and you carefully and mindfully take the first sip.

What was this like? Possibly awkward, unfamiliar, effortful? Possibly calming, interesting? Now ask yourself: *When was the last time I made my drink this way?* Usually, with everything from making a morning cup to helping kids with homework, our minds are scampering off to other times and other places.

WHAT IS MINDFULNESS?

Mindfulness means paying attention to what is happening in the present moment with curiosity, openness, and acceptance. Aperture awareness is a particular aspect of mindfulness.

We are capable of learning to observe our experiences as they are occurring, but it is not what we most naturally do. Much of the time our attention is elsewhere.

Matthew Killingsworth and Daniel Gilbert, research psychologists, studied our ability to attend to the present moment using a phone app to check in randomly on 2,250 volunteers to ask what they were doing. They found that the participants were not present 47 percent of their waking moments; their minds were "wandering" from what they were doing in the moment.

So, why are we so seldom in the present moment, the here and now? Roughly one hundred thousand years ago we developed the power of mental abstraction—the ability to be in the there and then. This ability turned out to have such enormous survival value that it became the primary way of using our big brains, and we became less skilled at simply perceiving what is happening in the moment.

Killingsworth and Gilbert also found that during those moments of "spacing out," the participants were not as happy as when their minds were focused on what they were doing. They summed it up: "A human mind is a wandering mind, and a wandering mind is an unhappy mind. The ability to think about what is not happening is a cognitive achievement that comes at an emotional cost."[1]

So, this overdeveloped tendency *not* to be in the present

moment costs us our happiness. It also costs us the ability to perceive and respond to what is presently happening with our partner.

Training in mindfulness, originally found in Buddhist meditation traditions circa 400 BC, has also been advocated by many Western teachers, psychologists, scholars, and practitioners. William James, often referred to as "the father of American psychology," said, "The faculty of voluntarily bringing back a wandering attention, over and over again, is the very root of judgment, character, and will." James advised "direct observation of one's own experience."[2] Many of the originators of psychotherapy, including Sigmund Freud, developed and taught "free floating attention" (another way of saying present moment awareness with acceptance) as the central practice of psychoanalysis and psychotherapy.

More recently, mindfulness has been widely recommended and taught by numerous practitioners, including Jon Kabat-Zinn with his Mindfulness-Based Stress Reduction (MBSR) program.[3] Kabat-Zinn developed this use of mindfulness at the University of Massachusetts Medical School to help patients with chronic illness and pain. Training in mindfulness has become widely available on sports teams and in children's classrooms, nursing homes, yoga classes, and workplaces including in the training of police and firefighters.

The Power of Present Moment Awareness

Mindful attention is our superpower for making changes. Mindful attention gives us the ability to change our health, our relationships, and even our brains.

Physics teaches us that as soon as we observe a phenomenon in the material world, we change it. This turns out to be true for awareness of our thoughts, feelings, and behavior as well—where changes can have powerfully positive effects on our relationships. With mindfulness we develop response flexibility, which helps us to be more of who we want to be: kind, loving, patient, understanding, and generous. These are not qualities we either have or do not have. We develop these qualities as we more closely observe our internal experiences—emotions, thoughts, motivations—and the external world of people we care about.

MINDFULNESS RESEARCH

We now have research on the effects of mindfulness and other types of awareness training on the structure and functioning of the brain, behavior and mental abilities, and health. Scientists working in this field would be quick to point out that more research is needed and that some findings are preliminary. Here's some of what's been found so far.

Mindfulness results in beneficial changes in brain regions related to:

- Attention
- Reactions to disturbing events
- Compassion and empathy
- Sense of self
- Self-regulation
- Reactions to pain

Mindfulness leads to behavioral and mental improvements in:

- Insight
- Impulse control

- Ability to distinguish narrative (interpretations of experience) from direct experience
- Response flexibility
- Working memory

Mindfulness can have physiological and health benefits, including:

- A decrease in recurrence of depression
- Lower levels of cortisol and cytokines (two indicators of stress levels)
- Less subjective stress in response to stress-provoking events
- Improvement of immune functions
- A shift toward resiliency in challenging situations[4]

Present moment awareness can be somewhat challenging, perhaps *very* challenging. This understanding itself is the starting place. Stephen Batchelor, an experienced mindfulness teacher, wrote, "Evasion of the unadorned immediacy of life is as deep-seated as it is relentless. Even with the ardent desire to be aware and alert in the present moment, the mind flings us into tawdry and tiresome elaborations of past and future. This craving to be otherwise, to be elsewhere, permeates the body, feeling, perceptions, will, consciousness itself."[5]

All the exercises in this book are exercises in mindfulness. Yes, they introduce you to behaviors that give you tools for better dialogues and better relationships. But most importantly they help you be aware and pay attention in new ways—mindfully.

Exercise: Socks Mindfulness

The next time you put on your socks, begin training your mind to focus on the present moment. As you reach for your socks, be aware of the various colors and textures. What are your choices? Notice that some socks please you more than others. As you retrieve the pair you will wear, feel them with your hands; you might even put them to your cheek and notice that socks feel different on cheeks than hands. Now you need to coax your feet into these chosen socks. Notice how you decide to do this. Will you sit down and make yourself comfortable for this next important moment in your day? Or will you stand and make it an interesting gymnastics balancing event? See if you can stay fully present as you complete this socks activity. *Reflect and write:*

- What was it like to put on your socks in this way?
- How was it different from the way you usually do it?
- What did you enjoy about it?
- What was hard or unpleasant about it?

Exercise: The Butterfly

Very often our attention is directed and purposeful. We pay attention to the clock on the wall to see if we are late. We look out the window to check the weather to know if we'll need a coat. We look for various items—keys, book, cell phone. This exercise, instead, promotes open attention, or simply observing what—of the myriad possibilities in this moment—catches your attention.

1. Practice this separately or with your partner for about fifteen minutes.
2. With your eyes closed, settle deeper into your chair and notice the weight of your body. Let the various sensations of sitting come to you in whatever way they do. In no particular order, you may notice the hardness or softness of the seat, the soles of your feet on the floor, the middle of your body and its state of hardness or softness, or other sensations.
3. Now turn your attention to the sounds that your ears are bringing to you. Can you hear the sounds themselves as distinct from the information they bring? What feels different in your body as you turn your attention to sound? Do you feel sounds in your body?
4. Finally, open your eyes and be curious about what catches the attention of your eyes. Think of yourself as a butterfly in a garden, flitting from one flower to the next or like a toddler as they explore a room, delighting in the various things that they find. What do you notice?
5. *Reflect and write:*

- What was this like for you?
- What did you enjoy?
- What was challenging?

6. *Discuss.*

SLOWING DOWN

Aperture awareness and mindfulness get easier when you slow

down. The pace of most conversations barely allows you to exchange information, much less sort through all the complex reactions and interactions. In any conversation, far more is happening than you can possibly be aware of in the moment. You're talking, listening, having memories, feeling emotions, and getting distracted. Things move fast, often without pauses or silences. Additionally, when emotions heighten, we tend to speed up—the opposite of what is needed.

Slowing things down gives you time to become aware of words, thoughts, feelings, and the opening and closing of apertures. In an interesting experiment, neuroscientist Vinod Menon tracked the thought patterns of people as they listened to music and found, surprisingly, that subjects' brains were actually more active during the pauses in the sound. Vinod says, "A pause is not a time where nothing happens."[6] Slowing down helps you modulate emotional arousal in conversation, but it can be harder than it sounds.[7] So, in this exercise, you'll be exaggerating the change in pace in order to feel the difference.

Exercise: Slowing Down

1. Choose a topic and set a timer for twenty minutes.
2. Begin your dialogue, but each time you speak, use only one or two sentences. Then, after one person has spoken, pause in silence for about thirty seconds—or approximately as long as the speaker was speaking. Then the next person will speak for one to two sentences. Then another pause. Eventually, you'll get a rhythm: speak . . . pause . . . speak . . . pause. It should feel a little like a rally in a tennis match. For much of the time, the ball is not being hit by either player; it

is in the air between them. And during that time, players are observing very carefully: watching the ball, watching the other player, getting their own body in position. This rhythm will probably feel strange, even awkward. You may be tempted to speak for longer or to omit the pauses, or both. Support each other in resisting this temptation. Hang in there, and let this slower pace help you to observe what's happening in the present moment.

3. Stop when the time is up. Don't continue the conversation.

4. *Reflect and write:*

- What was hard about this exercise?
- What did you like about it?
- What did you observe about the effects of the pace of the conversation?

5. *Discuss.*

COMMON REACTIONS TO THE SLOWING-DOWN EXERCISE

Every exercise has many possible outcomes. Here are some common reactions to this one and ideas about how to understand them.

1. *I didn't have enough time to finish explaining my thought.*
   It's true. Two sentences usually aren't enough, especially not at the beginning of a conversation.

But two paragraphs probably wouldn't be enough either. Usually what you're saying is complex. Some people have a pattern of talking so long that they overwhelm their partner or even themselves as they try to capture it all in one speaking turn.

We want so much to be understood! This exercise forces you to let go of trying to say it all at once, to realize that understanding comes gradually, and to acknowledge that much more is happening in your conversations than just the accumulation of information. Knowing that your partner will also speak briefly and you'll get to speak again soon, it may become easier and less uncomfortable to limit yourself. A new rhythm takes hold, one that relies less on finishing your thoughts and more on an active balance of listening and speaking.

2. *I hate just waiting during the silence.*
    Silence makes us uncomfortable. We're not used to it. It feels like something is wrong. It takes a while to learn that silence is not just a delay; it's a time to tune in. "First speak, then listen as the sound . . . cascades into silence," wrote William Isaacs, author of the book *Dialogue*.[8] "People typically notice that there is a notable change in the meaning of what they heard as they wait a moment or two and make space to let the meaning bloom."

You may find, in the silences, that in addition to

hearing more of the meanings of what your partner said, you're also able to hear the full meaning
of what *you've* just said. How often do you take
the time to do that?

3. *I didn't get so overwhelmed.*
   You may notice that you start to feel more relaxed
   and less overwhelmed. As you have more time to
   process, difficult conversations become easier and
   anxiety naturally diminishes.

Now let's look at how slowing down and mindfulness can
help you be aware of apertures and have better conversations.

FAST AND SLOW PROCESSING

As discussed in the previous chapter (see "Aperture and the
Limbic System" on page 34), our brains have two pathways for
processing incoming information, a fast track and a slow track.
The fast track is the "better safe than sorry" mechanism. The
slow track delivers more complex processing and more accuracy, but we have to wait for it.

For an experience of your fast and slow systems, try this experiment suggested by Nobel Prize winner Daniel Kahneman.[9]

Look at the picture on the next page.

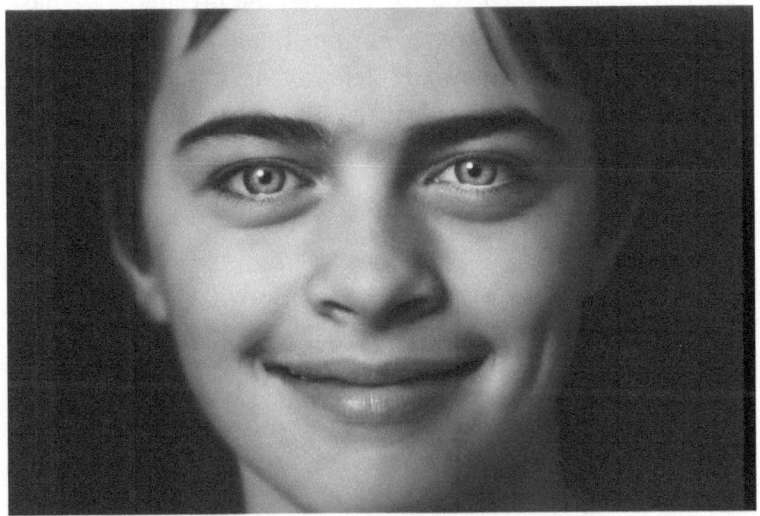

Credit: iStock, duncan1890

- What is this person feeling?
- How long did it take you to make that observation?
- How difficult did it feel?

Now look at and solve this math problem: (12 x 19)

- What is the answer?
- How long did it take you to get this answer?
- How difficult did it feel?

Reading faces uses your fast system; it's instantaneous and feels effortless. Math problems, even simple ones, require the slow system. They take longer, and you can feel yourself making an effort.

In conversations, your fast-track warning system can close your aperture before you even realize what's happening. Your partner says, "I don't like the way you're treating me," or "You didn't do what I asked you to," or even the dreaded "We have to talk." What happens next? For most of us, it's some combination of anxiety, dismay, and defensiveness. (*Defensiveness* is another term for closed aperture.) The immediate reaction in our nervous system might look like this.

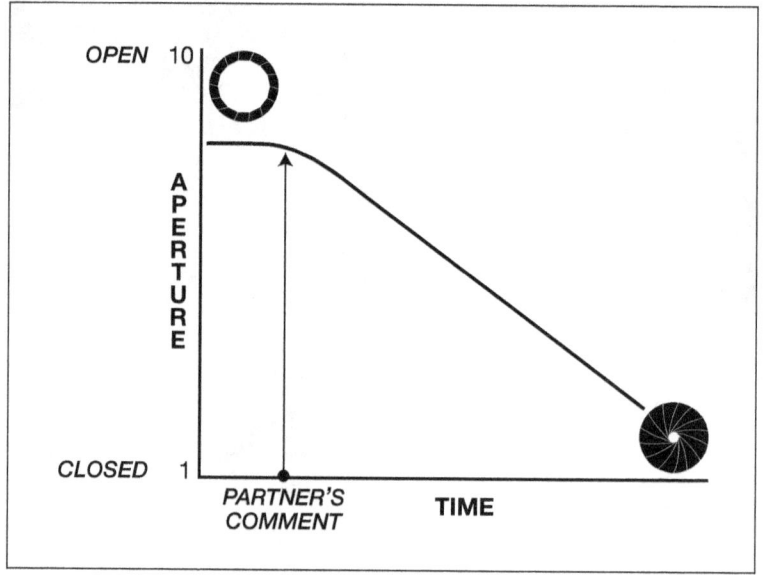

Figure 2: Aperture Closure

The defensive response (fast system, closed aperture) is not under your conscious control, which is why telling someone, "Don't get defensive!" usually makes things worse. It turns out that you cannot *not* get defensive; you can't negotiate with or control the fast system's closing response. The possibility for open apertures lies in understanding what to do next, once you notice your aperture, or your partner's, has closed.

When you learn to pause and give your slow system time to build a more nuanced understanding, you make room for a more considered response, one that's less likely to escalate conflict or trigger apertures to close. You can learn to delay your behavioral, verbal response until your second internal response, the one from your slow system, arrives.

For example, a fast-system response might sound something like: "Are you kidding me?! I most certainly was *not* the one who made us late to the party!" With a few seconds to reflect and return to open, it might sound more like "Wow, I'm surprised to hear you say that. I didn't even realize I was late."

Or if you hear, "It bums me out when you're too tired to speak to me when I get home," your fast response might be "Great. You try being with the kids all day and greeting me with a smile and dinner!" But after a pause to allow your aperture to recover, you might say, "Of course, it does. Let's talk later about what we can do differently."

If your relationship is in an upward spiral, the shift from closed to open might take only a few seconds. In a downward spiral, it will take longer, and your aperture may not completely open. But if you wait and observe closely, you will feel the initial closing response soften and pass. This makes all the difference in what happens next in your conversation.

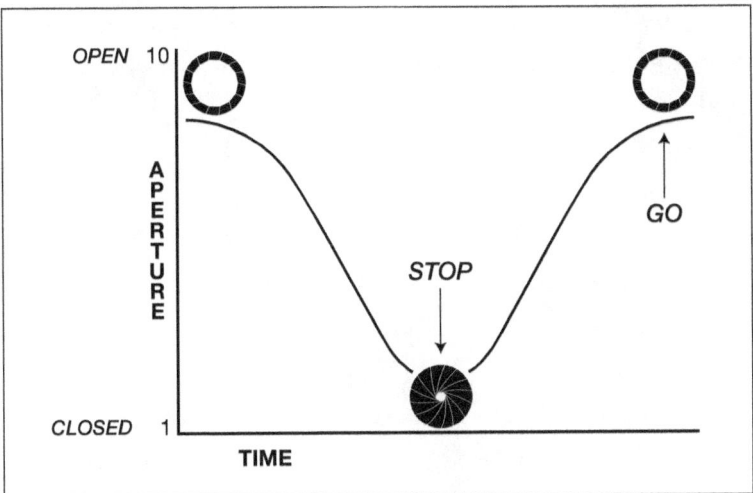

Figure 3: Aperture Closure and Recovery

Speaking with a closed aperture is likely to trigger a closed response in your partner. If they then respond from that closed position, defensiveness will likely escalate, eventually reaching a point where you are both closed.

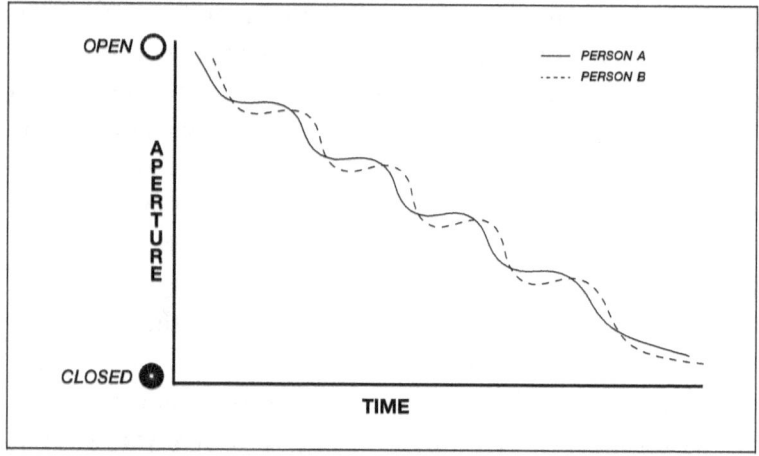

Figure 4: No Aperture Recovery: Both of You Increasingly Closed

On the other hand, in a conversation where both of you pause, waiting for the wave of defensiveness to pass and apertures to open again before speaking, the pattern of apertures might look like this.

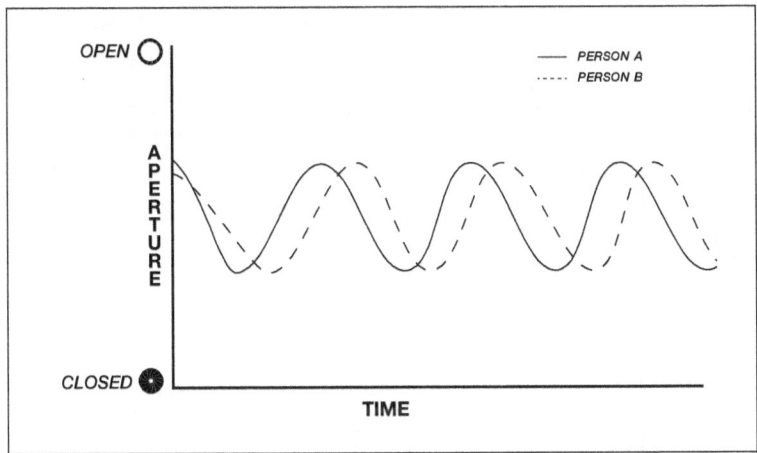

Figure 5: Riding the Waves, Apertures Recovering

Slowing down makes it easier to stay mindful and recover before speaking so that you maintain overall openness. You ride the waves of apertures closing to get back to open.

Exercise: Ride the Waves

Building on the skills from the exercises Aperture Awareness (page 32) and Slowing Down (page 55), you are going to experiment with paying close attention to the changes in your aperture each time your partner speaks. Sometimes, in response to what your partner says, your aperture will open; other times it will close. Maybe a little or maybe a lot.

If you notice that your apertures are stuck below 5, the conversation is probably too hard. You may need to try an easier topic. On the other hand, if your apertures are not closing at all, the two of you may be playing it too safe. You might try a harder topic or consider whether you can take more risks in the current one. (For more on taking risks in conversation, see "Working at Your Edge" on page 234.)

This exercise asks you to bring together your mindfulness and aperture awareness. Plan to spend some time with it, repeating it several times. Notice what's hard about it. Perhaps go back and practice more with the previous exercises, then return to this one. You're developing new abilities that can't be rushed. Take your time and be gentle with yourself and with each other.

1. Choose a topic and set the timer for twenty minutes.
2. Begin your dialogue and each time you speak, allow yourself only one or two sentences.
3. Then, each time your partner speaks, pay attention to your aperture. If your aperture closes in response to what you've heard, wait for the reopening. Speak only after you've felt your aperture open again. So, your pauses may be longer this time around. (If you find that your aperture does not reopen sufficiently to speak, 5 or better, you may want to discontinue this conversation. Perhaps try the exercise with an easier topic. In the next chapter you will learn more about working together to reopen.)
4. When the timer goes off, stop the conversation.
5. *Reflect and write:*

- How much time did your waves take to pass?
- Was it longer or shorter than you expected?
- What was it like to watch your reactions come and go?
- What was it like to wait for your partner's reactions to pass?
- Were you able to use this method to keep your apertures open over the course of the conversation?

- Were you able to notice the difference between your first and second responses?

6. *Discuss.*

If you find this exercise challenging, you're not alone. The instructions are deceptively simple: slow down and pay attention to apertures. But let's look closely at what's going on. You're attempting a complex set of shifts in behavior and attention. The exaggerated slowing down and the pauses are, themselves, challengingly different from usual conversations, requiring discipline and attention. In addition, you're practicing aperture awareness and trying to notice subtle shifts in your aperture. Finally, you are, possibly for the first time, practicing the new skill of observing moment-to-moment changes and waiting until a wave of aperture closure passes so that you are open enough to speak. All these skills involve mindfulness. If you are new to the practice of mindfulness, you may find this challenging. (Indeed, you may find it challenging even if you practice mindfulness regularly!)

Remember that mindfulness is simply a way of relating to all experience in an open, receptive way. At any time, during any activity, you can practice bringing your attention in this way to the present moment.

CHAPTER 3

What You Can Do with Aperture Awareness

When I first started focusing on aperture, I assumed that my clients would need to be taught to recognize this response in themselves and their partners. I quickly discovered that most people are sensing apertures already. In one session I watched as Sara and Raffe attempted to communicate. Sara was upset and trying to tell Raffe what was upsetting her. As she talked, his aperture began to close. The more he closed, the more she talked insistently, faster, and louder, and—as you might guess—the more she went on like this, the more closed he became. Finally, I interrupted her.

Me: Hold on a second. What do you see on his face?
Sara: Nothing, just blank as usual.
Me: Yes, and he's not even looking at you, right?
Sara: Right. That's what's so frustrating. He never even

looks at me or listens when I'm trying to talk about really important things.

Me: Would you describe him as closed or open right now?

Sara: Closed.

Me: So, if you noticed that he was closed, why did you keep talking?

Sara: I didn't know what else to do.

Eureka! I had just learned something very important about couples and aperture: We are very good at sensing our partner's aperture, as well as our own. We're just not very good at knowing what to do with this information.

Aperture awareness tells you when to slow down and stop in response to a closing aperture and when to move forward. Once we know what to do with aperture awareness, we become better at paying attention to it.

RESPONDING TO CLOSING APERTURES

Just as you can't have an intimate relationship without some conflicts and misunderstandings, you can't conduct a meaningful dialogue without aperture closures. So, let's talk about what to do when this happens.

What we want most in a conversation is to feel heard, understood, connected. This becomes increasingly unlikely as apertures close. In general, think of 5 or better as open enough to proceed. Apertures of less than 5 mean you are more likely to harm each other than to connect. As soon as either of you notices that someone's aperture is closing, especially if it's below 5, ask for a pause. You may sense apertures closing before you know why; trust that instinct. Pause to figure it out.

Continuing to talk when either of you is closed is not only ineffectual but sends the message that you are not interested in true dialogue. Proceeding with closed apertures decreases trust, and, like running a stop sign, it's likely to cause damage.

Closing apertures means that one of you is feeling vulnerable, or likely both of you are. An attempt to explore this will require yet more vulnerability. Try to provide your partner some reassurance of connection and caring, and some acknowledgment of your own vulnerability. Note that just by pausing the conversation you've already provided implicit reassurance that you are paying attention to your partner's aperture and your own, and that you care about them. Sometimes this is enough. Or you might add something like "I'm sorry you're not feeling comfortable" or "I want this to be a good conversation for both of us."

Once you're on solid ground again, try to determine what triggered closing and what might help reopen. Here's what Sara's conversation with Raffe might be if she focused on aperture:

> **Sara:** So, then you called to say you would be late, again. I'm just so exasperated with this happening all the time. I don't know what to do. I just can't stand it anymore!
>
> **Raffe:** [Silent and looking away.]
>
> **Sara:** [Pauses.] I'm not sure what's going on, but I feel like you're shutting down.
>
> **Raffe:** [A brief pause.] Yeah, I probably am.
>
> **Sara:** Like maybe a 4?
>
> **Raffe:** [Looks at her.] Probably a 4 going toward a 3.
>
> **Sara:** [Takes a moment to consider her own aperture and reopen.] What can I do differently?
>
> **Raffe:** Well, I've told you I really don't like it when you exaggerate, like when you say I do this "*all* the

time." Also, when you say things like "I just can't stand it anymore," it makes me feel very insecure, like you could just leave me or something. I'm trying to hang in there, but if you could tone it down a bit . . .

Sara: Okay, I get it. Of course, I'm not going to leave you. I guess I'm pretty pissed at you. Sorry, let me see if I can say this differently. [She pauses, noticing that he seems to be reopening.] Are you ready to try again?

Raffe: Yeah, I'm back to a 5.

Notice Sara's attention to Raffe's aperture, the pause when she sees that he's closing, the reassurance, and the request for information. Often if you pause as soon as you sense closure, a little reassurance and information will be enough to get you back on track. If things have shut down more dramatically, you may need a longer pause, more reassurance, and more exploration.

And, of course, because of limbic resonance, the most effective thing you can do to help your partner reopen is to open your own aperture. This involves skills in internal self-management, which we will discuss in more detail in Part Three (page 163).

APERTURE AWARENESS FOR HARD CONVERSATIONS

- Keep track of apertures: yours and your partner's.
- Pause for any aperture below 5.
- Reassure.
- Inquire.

• Return to the content only when both apertures are 5 or better.

Exercise: Aperture Recovery

If you feel ready, this would be a good time to choose a new topic, perhaps a slightly harder one. Expect to do each of these next two exercises several times (using the same topic each time or different ones), with lots of patience for your own learning and your partner's.

1. Allow a half hour for this conversation.
2. In this conversation you will pause every ten minutes to inquire about aperture and record each of your apertures. In addition, you will pause anytime you sense someone's aperture closing. If at any check-in either aperture is below 5 or has fallen significantly since the last check-in pause, reassure and inquire. Do not resume the conversation until both of you are at 5 or above.
3. Set the timer for ten minutes and begin your conversation.
4. At each check-in record the following:

• Your sense of your aperture _____
• Your sense of your partner's aperture _____
• Your partner's sense of their aperture _____
• Your partner's sense of your aperture _____

5. *Reflect and write:*

- What reassurances did you offer?
- What reassurances did your partner offer?
- What did you learn about what caused apertures to close?
- What did you do to help apertures reopen?
- What else did you learn?

6. *Discuss.*

If you find that neither of your apertures is ever falling below 5, you may be playing it too safe. For some couples, this is a familiar pattern. If, in this exercise, you did not get enough practice with aperture closure, you may need to change the topic, find an aspect of the topic that's more challenging, or take more risks as you go along. Talk to each other about what you might do to move toward a more challenging conversation. Then repeat the exercise.

On the other hand, if you found it hard to have any part of the conversation with apertures of 5 or better, you might:

- Choose a less challenging topic.
- Review Slowing Down (page 55) and Ride the Waves (page 63).
- Take a look at Part Three, especially Chapter 9 (page 180).

Then come back and try again.

RESPONDING TO OPENING APERTURES

Relationships grow when each of you is willing to risk offering more and asking for more. When it comes to building intimacy and trust, moving forward on green is just as important as stopping on red. When your partner signals an open aperture, you must be able to sense it and respond. Not doing so may be experienced as rejection. When one person misses a cue and fails to approach, a moment of potential closeness evaporates.

In a downward spiral, if one of you tentatively risks some vulnerable or tender feelings, the other may fail to notice—or even distrust it. Aperture awareness helps you pick up on signals (sometimes small) of willingness to trust. Awareness of your own aperture enables you to recognize your hesitancy, acknowledge it, and consider risking a bit and moving forward—an example of mindfulness creating response flexibility.

Let's look at an example of such a moment without aperture awareness. Della and Charles are discussing a particularly difficult period in raising their son.

Charles: Remember when he got pulled over by the police for running a stop sign? (5)

Della: Yeah, and you keep reminding me that I was "nowhere to be found." (5)

Charles: I just meant it was hard that I couldn't reach you. (5)

Della: Really, we're going there again!? (4)

Charles: [His face changes, softens, and his chin starts to quiver.] I just feel so alone sometimes. (7)

Della: Yep, here we go again—blame Della! (3)

Charles: [Stiffens.] Okay! Whatever! (2)

With more aperture awareness:

Charles: Remember when he got pulled over by the police for running a stop sign? (5)

Della: Yeah, and you keep bringing it up that I was "nowhere to be found." (5)

Charles: [With some softening.] It was hard that I couldn't reach you. (6)

Della: [Pauses, studying him; her face partly open.] (5)

Charles: [His face changes, softens more noticeably, and his chin starts to quiver.] I just feel so alone sometimes. (7)

Della: [Pauses, notices how she wants to close but sees his openness.] I get it. I guess I'm not quite ready to be sympathetic, but I'm sure that's true. (6)

Charles: [Cries softly with his eyes averted, then wipes his cheeks and looks up.] Okay. (6)

In the first version, they reenacted the same injuries they'd felt the first time around—and confirmed their worst fears. In the second, though it may take more than one such conversation to reverse being guarded and angry, they managed to stay open and avoid reinjuring each other.

Exercise: Go on Green

Use your topic from the previous exercise, Aperture Recovery (page 70).

1. Set the timer for a half hour and begin your conversation.
2. You are looking for moments when you can offer your partner a bit more openness and moments when your partner is offering you an opening. When you notice these moments, slow things down enough to verify your perceptions. If you think you see your partner trying to be more open, ask. If you are trying to be more open and your partner doesn't seem to see this, tell them.

Your conversation will shift back and forth between the topic and shorter conversations about these signals of openness. As always, if apertures are closing—and especially if they are falling below 5—return to the strategies of Aperture Recovery (page 70).

3. *Reflect and write:*

- What was it like for you to be looking for your partner's openings?
- How well were you able to respond to these?
- What was it like for you to risk opening a bit more?
- How did your partner respond to your openings?
- How did it go when you tried to exchange information about these times?
- What else did you learn?

4. *Discuss.*

HELPING EACH OTHER KEEP OPEN APERTURES

Perhaps you're starting to get a sense of the intricate dance of apertures that's happening all the time, whether you're aware or not. With aperture awareness (and with mindfulness in general) we become able to participate in more intentional ways.

You sense your partner's aperture closing, and you feel your own hesitancy. So, you wait a moment, and you find a little courage. Your aperture reopens a bit, and you turn to her with a smile. Your partner sees the smile, and she is momentarily confused. *What does this smile mean? Aren't we fighting? Is this a green light?* She finds a bit of hopefulness and smiles back. You both relax a bit, perhaps breathe a sigh of relief. Apertures open a bit more, and you both feel a little hopeful.

With aperture awareness, you no longer have to get stuck in adversarial interactions where "the best defense is a good offense." The change may be disorienting; even your best defenses and offenses are of no use. They don't get you the connection you long for. In fact, they don't even keep you safe. Safety in intimacy comes from helping the other person to feel safe. If your partner feels threatened, their aperture will close. When your partner is closed, you don't get heard and understood. In an intimate relationship, we must do everything possible to help our partner maintain an open aperture. The most powerful tool you have to that end is your own open aperture.

Exercise: Helping Each Other Keep Open Apertures

First, read the vignette below. Then go back over this exchange and mark the times when either Hanna or Julie did something that helped the other open their aperture. You could do this exercise in tandem, with discussion at the end, or do it together, discussing as you go.

> **Hanna:** Can we go over your travel schedule again?
> **Julie:** Why? I've already told you what I know, and I don't have that much control over it.
> **Hanna:** I know, but it would help me to go over it again while I'm looking at a calendar.
> **Julie:** [Exasperated sigh, dirty look.]
> **Hanna:** [Tightness creeping into her voice.] It doesn't have to be now, but soon would be good.
> **Julie:** [Wearily.] Now is as good as any time, I guess.

Hanna: How about I make us a cup of tea and we meet at the table in ten minutes.

[Ten minutes and a couple of sips of tea later.]

Julie: Sorry I was so cranky. I'm tired, and I'm tired of traveling for work. And I know you hate it too.

Hanna: Yep, I do. Still, it's easier when I have a clear idea of what's coming up. Thanks for calming down.

[As they review, Julie senses Hanna getting tense as they discuss the fourth trip in as many weeks. Julie pauses, reaches across the table to pat Hanna's hand.]

Julie: Babe, I know this sucks.

Hanna: [Suddenly angry.] No, I don't think you do know. How could you know when you're never here? I'm just a pit stop for you!

[They both sit silently with clenched jaws for a few minutes.]

Julie: Maybe we need to talk again about whether me having this job is working out the way we hoped.

Hanna: [Looks up, a bit misty-eyed.] I don't know. I'm not sure what to do. But I feel too alone here.

Julie: I don't think you've ever said it that way. We need a bigger conversation about this. Let's stop for now and plan to revisit this soon. How about a walk before dinner?

BASELINE APERTURE: EMPHASIZING THE POSITIVE

Though much of this book focuses on working with apertures during a particular moment or conversation, remember that your aperture is operating all the time, even as you're reading the paper together or just walking around the house. Couples have a baseline aperture. As events and conversations unfold, apertures open or close from this starting place. In an upward spiral, the baseline aperture is open; in a downward spiral it's closed. This section is about influencing that baseline aperture in positive ways.

Pulling weeds is not enough to create a beautiful garden; you also have to plant flowers. It's the same with couples: fixing the problems is important, but assuring you have plenty of positive experiences together is the foundation of trust and connection. And this foundation is your starting place for dealing with the problems.

This is one of the ways that the brain's default functioning does not always serve us. The brain's first job is survival—we're wired to look for threats, and so we're more alert for negative experiences than for positive. When it comes to building relationships, we can use mindfulness to override this tendency and notice and benefit from the positive moments.

Many positives go unnoticed or get taken for granted in the life of a couple. Your partner was careful not to wake you when she had to get up early for a meeting. Dinner was ready for you when you got home. He called the plumber. She stopped at the nursery to get the birdseed. She got her hair done and a new dress for dinner with your boss. Every day there are favors, kindnesses, help in the business of daily life.

When we take these things for granted, we forget that having a partner is a gift. Our efforts to grow together must include appreciating the everyday gestures that sustain us.

Exercise: Positive Acknowledgment

1. Over the next week, make at least three positive comments each day on something your partner

did that you liked or appreciated. These can be big or small things, but the appreciation must be explicit. *Thanks for bringing in the trash cans. I like your new shirt. Great that you remembered to stop for milk on the way home. Thanks so much for changing your business dinner so that we could keep our date night.* As you do this, you may start to notice how many good things in your relationship were passing by without notice or acknowledgment.

2. *Reflect and write:*

- What was hard about this exercise?
- What was surprising about this exercise?
- What did you learn?

3. *Discuss.*

LOVE LIVES ON TIME

There is no substitute for spending time together. In *A General Theory of Love*, authors Thomas Lewis, Fari Amini, and Richard Lannon emphasize that "love lives on time. . . . Relatedness is a physiologic process that, like digestion or bone growth, admits no plausible acceleration."[1] We often expect our relationships to thrive, even as we squeeze them into ever-smaller spaces. The supreme value in modern life is speed. We want everything instantly. We find ways to do things more quickly and trick ourselves into thinking we can do several things at once, ignoring all evidence to the contrary.

I often meet with couples who are not spending any time together. They don't make time for date night, catching up at the end of the day, making plans, or for the many other things couples need time together for. Their relationship is in serious trouble, yet the better relationship they want can only happen if they have time together. And, of course, as things become harder and less fun, spending time together becomes unappealing, even hazardous! At that point, the motivation to find time for each other in busy schedules is zero.

As with a lot of things, you're not going to make time for each other just because you *should*. In Part Two, you're going to learn ways to make your time together less difficult and more satisfying.

GOTTMAN'S SIX HOURS

John Gottman has described the essential six hours a week needed for relationship health:

1. **Partings:** Two minutes at the start of each workday to connect briefly before heading out. (Ten minutes a week.)
2. **End-of-day check-in:** A twenty-minute talk to catch up with each other. (One hour forty minutes per week.)
3. **Admiration and appreciation:** Find a way to compliment your partner every day, to show that you appreciate them—a five-minute task, seven days a week. (Thirty-five minutes per week.)
4. **Affection:** Show physical affection for your partner. Hug, pat, kiss, touch. Gottman specifically advises goodnight kisses! Five minutes a day, seven days a week. (Thirty-five minutes per week.)
5. **Weekly date:** This is the big one, timewise. Gottman allows for two hours, once per week, to

connect, chat, dream, plan, and enjoy each other's
company.

6. **Weekly conversation about the relationship:**
    This is the weekly dialogue described on
    page 111.[2]

PART TWO

Dialogue

Real jamming goes like this: you begin to feel
your way to an interpretation of this piece;
you hear your neighbor feeling her way to
a different one. You listen hard as you play.
She listens hard as she plays. Gradually, or
suddenly, as you play you begin to hear the
special magic of what she is doing and you
begin to relate your interpretation to hers.
Simultaneously she is hearing you and relating her interpretation to yours. And now the
group's interpretation is not anyone's—it is
everyone's. It would be difficult to say who
started what or who thought up which part.

—Michael Kahn, PhD[1]

CHAPTER 4

What Is Dialogue?

Conversation is a major creative force in intimate relationships. We exchange information, ideas, hopes, dreams, fears, and sadnesses. We make plans, large and small. We entertain each other with humor and originality. We want comfort, advice, validation, patience, and pleasure. We want so much from our conversations and are constantly reminded how hard this is.

Your conversations, especially the hard ones, determine a great deal about your relationship. You may or may not solve a problem, come to consensus, or feel good afterward, but with every interaction you have a chance to affect your relationship for better or worse. Each conversation sets the stage for the next one, and a good conversation creates positive expectations of trust, understanding, and intimacy.

Dialogue is a specific kind of conversation in which the priorities are *relationship*, *learning*, and *collaboration*. Open apertures and aperture awareness make dialogue possible, and conversations that are dialogues lead to open apertures.

Dialogue is quite different from conversations that feature an exchange of information and opinions, aimed at figuring out who is right and whether we agree or disagree. In *The Tao of Conversation*, Michael Kahn writes:

> We are a fight culture. We glory in competition, and we want to win. Our best sellers carry titles like *Winning Through Intimidation*. We treat our elections as boxing matches, and our national leaders unhesitatingly set race against race and class against class. Our highways and city streets have become racetracks filled with angry competitors. At home, we entertain ourselves with television humor built around the putdown.[1]

Kahn goes on to say that in such a culture it can seem that "combative or disengaged are the only available conversational modes." Recently I was working with a couple, encouraging Jan to be bolder, more direct, about what she wanted from Ellen. She was extremely reluctant. Finally, frustrated with all my urgings, she blurted out, "I don't want to *force* her to agree with me!" And there you have it. Jan saw only two options: to keep quiet about it, or to force the other person to change. One winner, one loser.

Without intending to, we often conduct our conversations like medieval jousts, in which the goal is to vanquish the other and avoid being harmed. In this climate, the more aggressive among us fight to win. Those who are squeamish about bloodletting opt instead for disengagement.

I recently sat with Laura and Mitch in a difficult conversation. Mitch was trying very hard, in multiple creative ways, to convince Laura of his point of view. The harder he tried, the more she closed. Both were becoming extremely frustrated. I asked them to pause, then I turned to him and said, "It seems as if you are trying to convince her."

He quickly agreed. I suggested that convincing is a very risky business. He looked at me with astonishment. "But that's what I'm good at; that's what I do. Why would it be risky?"

When you find yourself arguing for your position or trying to convince the other person that you are right, you sacrifice the relationship, your learning, and the benefits of collaboration. I would say that makes convincing significantly risky.

THE CHALLENGE OF DIFFERENT REALITIES

In addition to these cultural biases, we have psychoneurological biases that make dialogue difficult. Knowing what these are and how to work with them will help you succeed at keeping them from getting in the way of dialogue. Consider the following:

- Our perceptions and memories are subjective and often inaccurate.
- We have a vast capacity to ignore our ignorance.
- We experience a sense of certainty of our subjective experience.
- We ignore information that contradicts our beliefs.[2]

Studies from perceptual psychology have demonstrated many aspects of our difficulties in knowing, perceiving, recording, and remembering experience. In studies of eyewitness reports of crimes, researchers found that witnesses' descriptions

are frequently inaccurate and quite different from one another.[3] Furthermore, the research of Kevin Dunbar has suggested
that we actually have a "delete key" in the brain that's triggered when we encounter information at odds with our beliefs.
He watched this area light up when scientists encountered
data inconsistent with their expectations and noted that the
scientists often had no memory later of having perceived the
discrepant information.[4] As early as 1957 Leon Festinger published his research showing that when confronted with ideas
that seem contradictory, or dissonant, we get very uncomfortable and try to find some way to resolve this tension.[5]

Knowing is more comfortable than not knowing. So much
so that we have an astonishing capacity to ignore our ignorance. Furthermore, we attempt to create certainty at the expense of accuracy.[6] People often end up predicting the worst
and acting on that prediction, simply because it's easier to
know that something bad is coming than to endure the uncertainty of not knowing. On top of that, being wrong is uncomfortable and often comes with a sense of deflation and
embarrassment. In our competitive culture, being wrong is
often the equivalent of losing.

Because the ability to act is so important to our survival,
we are hardwired with something called *egocentric bias*.[7] This
means that we experience an automatic belief that we are
right. It's as if our brains insist on us feeling confident in their
infallibility and accuracy. Great for running from the saber-
toothed tiger or catching a baseball; not so great for collaborating with other humans about the subtler aspects of reality.
In other words, our perceptions and memories are subjective
and inaccurate, and we have a sense of certainty that these
perceptions are "right."

Now comes the really interesting part. Part of our secu-
rity comes from trusting our own flawed perceptions, and part
of it comes from experiencing shared reality: We tacitly agree

to agree with each other about the way things are. All social connections rely on these tacit agreements. Some are explicit and widely held, like the rules of the road that allow us to drive safely. Others, more subtle and implicit, define membership in particular groups, like agreements on what constitutes social fairness.

When our partner has an experience that differs from ours, we feel threatened. In trying to satisfy both our need to be certain and our need for shared reality, we escalate our assertions and try to extract agreement. So often, conversations about things trivial or important begin with one person describing something that happened and the other, usually with mild to severe discomfort, saying, "Wait a minute, that's not at all what happened!" The debate is launched.

The combination of flawed perceptions, egocentric bias, and the need for shared reality creates moments of tension, fear, or anger when, as is so often the case, someone important to us has a different experience. No wonder there is frequently more heat than light when couples discuss what is going on.

Exercise: Different Realities

This exercise is about experiencing simple differences in perception.

1. When you are both ready, set a timer for twenty seconds and look at the image in Appendix C (page 271). Don't look at it before then!
2. Close the book and each write a quick paragraph describing what you saw in as much detail as possible.
3. Without looking at the image, spend a few minutes comparing your versions of what you saw.

What was the same? Which parts did you remember differently? Which did only one of you see? Pay special attention to your sense of certainty about your version, and to any reaction you have to the differences in your accounts. What do you feel as you learn that your partner remembers certain details differently than you do?

4. Now open the page again and compare your descriptions to the actual image. What did you see accurately? What did you misremember? Which things did you not see at all?

5. *Reflect and write.*

6. *Discuss.*

THE THREE PRIORITIES OF DIALOGUE

So, how can we shift from a contentious potential argument to a true dialogue? Let's begin with an understanding of the three priorities of dialogue: relationship, learning, and collaboration.

Relationship

In our individualistic culture, we're used to the idea that getting our needs met means standing up for ourselves, putting ourselves first. We negotiate with each other and assume that a good relationship is based on fairness, compromise, and quid pro quo. But this is a mistake. A relationship with a balance of wins and losses is still an adversarial relationship, albeit a civilized one. This isn't really good enough, and it isn't all that is possible.

So, what's the alternative? For most couples, the quality of the relationship is the most important determinant of happiness and well-being. If we are on good terms with our partner, everything else feels better. In the Harvard Grant Study, a seventy-five-year longitudinal study of 268 physically and mentally healthy male Harvard graduates, George Valliant found that loving, supportive relationships were more important to happiness than a successful career, money, or good health.[8] In other words, taking care of the relationship is the most important thing we can do to take care of ourselves.

A common misunderstanding is that putting the relationship first is the same as putting the other first. Though the ability to do this when needed is valuable, it's not the same thing as putting the relationship first. When you're taking care of the relationship, you're making sure that *both* of you know what *each* of you wants, needs, and cares about. You then figure out what is best for your couple. Sometimes this does mean you decide to feature your partner's needs; other times it means you decide to feature your own needs.

Putting the relationship first means we learn to view everything, especially our difficult moments, through the lens of "What's good for the relationship?" In dialogue, this means that the impact of the conversation on the relationship is held as the most important outcome.

Learning

In dialogue, you prioritize learning. This means learning from the perceptions and understandings that you each came to the conversation with. You mindfully get beyond your need to be right, bringing your uncertainty, which Maggie Jackson, in *Uncertain*, calls "the very cognitive capacity that most broadens our mental horizons."[9]

Beyond this, you are partners in exploring to discover things that *neither* of you knew before the conversation. The most important thing you bring to dialogue is your curiosity, your questions. Esther Perel, therapist and relationship expert, says, "A good question . . . disrupts a pattern. It goes deeper. Sometimes, it goes sideways. It enables us to travel to a new place without ever leaving one another's side."[10] One sure sign that you are *not* in dialogue is that your conversation has no surprises. A conversation in which you know exactly what each of you is going to say is not dialogue.

As Peter Senge, known for his work on learning organizations and systems thinking, wrote, "If we can simply observe without forming conclusions as to what our observations mean and allow ourselves to sit with all the seemingly unrelated bits and pieces of information we see, fresh ways to understand a situation can eventually emerge."[11] Dialogue is discovery. Most importantly, in dialogue we discover each other and we discover ourselves. Learning is so important to this process that Part Four is dedicated to it.

Collaboration

Dialogue is a conversation in which you are collaborating. You're both committed to a learning-based exchange that has a positive effect on the relationship. The collaboration of dialogue involves trusting that, with openness, you can make the most of your ability to connect. In dialogue you do not own and defend points of view. Instead, you each bring to the conversation anything you feel may be helpful, and you work to find the relevance and contribution of your partner's ideas as well as your own.

Collaboration implies a dependency on each other for exploration, and an openness to being influenced. The process can be challenging for our sense of autonomy. Or, as William Isaacs wrote in *Dialogue*, "It is actually counterproductive, the skeptics might argue, to get too close to one another's thoughts. To do so is to risk losing our objectivity, our distance, our cherished beliefs."[12] We've learned to armor ourselves for conversations—a battle of ideas and wills. In that context, changing our minds or being influenced is tantamount to defeat. Yet John Gottman's research shows that one indicator of a lasting relationship is a willingness to be influenced by the other.[13] An open aperture is the beginning of that willingness.

THE IMPORTANCE OF NOT KNOWING

Mindfulness makes it possible to tolerate the discomfort of not knowing, and of knowing differently than our partner. In fact, the state of not-knowing and uncertainty is a prerequisite for learning. Descriptions of creative and intuitive states converge on a state of awareness that is receptive, diffuse, paralogical, risky, and playful. Or, as Keats said, "being in uncertainties, mysteries, doubts, without any irritable reaching after facts and reason."[14] Not knowing, being wrong, and changing are often mistaken for weakness. Yet, if you think about it, these are absolute preconditions for learning. "Pay special attention to getting lost," Naomi Newman, psychotherapist and playwright, says. "If you're not lost, you're in trouble. If you know where you're going, you're going somewhere you've been before, and what's the point of that?"[15]

Exercise: Awareness of the Preference for Knowing

Dialogue is a continuous experiment with uncertainty and difference. The first step is tuning in and acknowledging your preference for certainty, your egocentric bias, and your need for shared reality. The following exercise, which is a private exploration of your own thoughts and feelings, will point you in this direction. The goal is to discover your experiences of knowing and not knowing.

1. Sit quietly with your notebook. Think of a topic that is very hard for you and your partner to talk about.

2. Notice how you feel about discussing this with your partner. These feelings may show up as emotions or as physical sensations. Anxiety and tension may be experienced as a tightness some-where in your body. Discouragement could feel like a heaviness or lack of energy. Record these feelings.

3. What might the two of you disagree about in this conversation? What do you think/believe related to this topic? What does your partner think/believe? How certain are you that you are right? Notice and record what it feels like to have this certainty or uncertainty.

4. How does it feel to imagine that your partner does not agree with you? Can you imagine yourself try-ing to convince your partner that you are right? Can you now imagine a way to talk about this without trying to persuade your partner?

5. What did you learn?

CHAPTER 5

Cultivating the Skills of Dialogue

Earlier, I likened apertures to breathing. Each goes on without our awareness, and we can learn to identify and modulate both in helpful ways. Conversation is like this too. It's such a basic aspect of who we are socially that much of it happens outside our awareness. We talk without thinking, without choosing, without considering the effect of our words or our motivation for saying them. In some ways, it's like talking in our sleep. And there is so much to be aware of—apertures opening and closing, emotions arising, what we say and what we hear, and the stories we're telling ourselves underneath all that. The most important skill for dialogue is awareness.

In this chapter, you'll learn how to become more aware in conversation and what you can do with this increased ability. You'll learn more about when to talk, when to listen, and how to begin and end. Each dialogue is an opportunity for you to experiment with changing something simple about the way you talk to each other, and then to observe how this change affects the quality of the conversation. Keep in mind as you proceed that the most important outcome of any conversation is the effect on your relationship.

SPEAKING, LISTENING, AND BALANCE

Speaking in dialogue is an act of leadership. When we are in the speaker role, we are in the driver's seat. The speaker directs the attention of the other along a certain path. They are guiding thoughts and feelings and affecting apertures. As with all good leadership, this involves a humble appreciation of the responsibility and careful attention to the input of the followers. Too often we speak without considering the effects of our speech on the listeners. This is an abdication of leadership and recklessness with the power of speech. We would consider it foolish and dangerous to drive a car blindfolded, and yet we often engage in conversation in this way.

To speak well, you must first be able to listen to yourself, to all that is going on inside you. Your feelings and openness will shape the way your partner hears your words. The more you are aware of this, the better you will communicate.

Another important aspect of speaking that often gets ignored has to do with the need to orient your listener, and yourself, as to your intent. The implicit question "Why are you telling me this?" is always there. We communicate better when we provide some information about this as we speak. We may be speaking to reassure, to be understood, to highlight differences, or for a variety of other objectives.

Even more challenging than the leadership of speaking well is the followership of listening well. Listening may be the best gift we can give each other. Esther Perel says, "One of the most powerful ways for people not to feel deeply alone is for them to feel listened to."[1]

And yet listening is hard. Jacques Barzun, historian and philosopher of education, writes, "Listening seems to be the hardest thing in the world and misunderstanding the easiest. . . . In a lifetime one is lucky to meet six or seven people who know how to attend."[2]

We can all think faster than we can talk—in fact, about four times faster.[3] As we try to listen, our brain races ahead in many directions at once. Not realizing this, we sometimes find ourselves thinking we're smarter than the person speaking. So, listening, too, requires humility. We must submit to the pace and pattern of the other person's speech, and this will never be identical to our own preferred patterns of listening. We must watch for the patterns of *their* thought and follow where they lead. We must be careful not to predict what's coming next or to hear what we were expecting instead of what was said. We must question our assumptions and reactions and not guard our own ideas too vigilantly.

All of this gets harder when the topic is uncomfortable or high stakes. When we're upset, limbic arousal increases and the amount of oxygen and glucose available for cortical and precortical functioning decreases; basically, this means our information processing slows. One study found that just looking at a frowning face could cause us to process more slowly than looking at a smiling face. When this happens, apertures close, and we become more likely to respond negatively, make false connections, and misinterpret. With limbic arousal our attention is drawn inward, away from the speaker, and our ability to listen and process is drastically compromised.[4]

Good dialogue draws on the wisdom of both participants. Each must be able to speak and listen. In many couples, one person has an easier time talking and the other is more comfortable listening, especially when it comes to difficult conversations. Over time, this difference may increase as you settle into a pattern—one person doing most of the talking, and the other, most of the listening. This may be comfortable or, at times, a source of frustration. But even when it's comfortable, it rarely supports good dialogue.

This polarization of roles compromises exploration and learning. Too much talking by one person can get in the way of the quieter person learning how to express themselves with words and valuing what they have to say. Conversely, when the quieter person does not speak up, the talker doesn't have much opportunity to become a better listener.

In addition to how much each person speaks, there are other types of balance that influence dialogue. In one conversation, a man said to his partner, "It's not that I don't like your ideas or want to hear them, but your intensity sometimes makes it hard for me to know and express what I think." The balance of intensity is another aspect of balance that is important to dialogue.

Other types of balance may be individual to your partnership. Experimenting with the balance of time spent talking changes conversations significantly and leads to awareness of other important aspects of balance.

Exercise: Speaking and Listening

This exercise is designed to help you become more aware of your roles as speaker and listener. You will need about ten minutes. You will not choose a topic; each speaker will use their allotted time to say whatever they most want their partner to hear, on any subject. (This exercise is adapted from one I learned thanks to Ellyn Bader and Peter Pearson.)

1. Choose one partner to be the first speaker and set a timer for three minutes. The speaker uses their time however they wish. The listener's role in this

exercise is just that: listen, no talking whatso-
ever. This is not active listening, where you might
encourage, ask questions, nod, say, "Hmm," et
cetera. This is silent listening.

2. When the timer goes off, the speaker stops immediately, even in the middle of a sentence. Then
wait a minute for both of you to digest what has
been said before switching roles.

3. Set the timer for three minutes for the second
speaker. Their task is a bit harder because it's
difficult not to respond to what you've just heard.
Instead, the second speaker should use their three
minutes to talk about whatever is most important
to them.

4. *Reflect and write:*

- What was each role like for you?
- Was one easier than the other?
- How was it to speak within this structure?
- Was it easier or harder to listen when that was
  your only task?
- What did you notice about leadership and
  followership?
- What else did you notice or learn during the
  exercise?

5. When you are finished, *do not* discuss what was
said for at least an hour. Plan to spend that time
apart so that each of you can pay attention to your
unfolding reactions. At the end of that hour, write
a few notes about how your thoughts and feelings
evolved after the exercise.

6. *Discuss.*

Exercise: Balance

Awareness is the key to adjusting balance as needed. In the following exercise you will start with describing what you know about your usual patterns of talking and listening. Then you will proceed to practice balance in a twenty-minute conversation.

1. Before beginning your dialogue, spend a few
    minutes thinking about and writing about the
    following:

    •   What percentage of the time in a typical conver-
        sation are you talking?
    •   What percentage are you listening?
    •   As you try to move toward more balance, what do
        you think will be the challenges for you?
    •   What will be the challenges for your partner?

2. Briefly discuss. (Note: If balance is particularly
    difficult, or if you suspect that it may be, you
    can repeat Slowing Down from page 55 for extra
    practice.)
3. Using one of your topics, proceed to dialogue for
    about twenty minutes, paying careful attention
    to the balance of speaking and listening. In fact,
    whoever tends to listen more should be speaking
    at least 51 percent of the time.
4. *Reflect and write:*

    •   What did you notice about leadership and
        followership?

- What did you need to adjust in your participation to achieve balance?

5. *Discuss.*

THE VALUE OF SPEAKING IN SHORTER BITS

Couples often have a pattern where one or both of them speak for too long. When both of them have this pattern, conversations are a sequence of monologues rather than real dialogue. Speaking vulnerably is risky. We want to be understood and responded to, and we're also afraid of what the response—especially in difficult conversations—might be. Sometimes people keep speaking because of this fear.

The other thing that may be going on is that one person needs more time to put their thoughts into words. The other person—the more comfortable talker—mistakes this slower pace for their partner not having something to say or, worse yet, assumes they are withholding something. Silence can be uncomfortable. Rather than waiting and allowing time for their partner to respond, the talker often just keeps talking, sometimes repeating themselves.

Yet a third pattern of talking too long is that the "talker," usually without realizing it, develops the habit of carrying the whole conversation—speaking their part and the other's too. What's needed is simply to "Let the words cascade into silence."[5]

Exercise: Speaking in Shorter Bits

This exercise is a repeat of Slowing Down, from page 55, but this time, instead of one to two sentences, you will speak in short paragraphs, more like five to seven sentences.

1. Choose a topic, set a timer for twenty minutes, and decide who will begin.
2. Each time you speak, use about six sentences. Then pause for about as long as the time spent speaking. Then the other person speaks for about a paragraph. Continue like this for the twenty minutes.
3. Use the silences to observe. What is it like to speak? Are you concerned about the response—or lack of response—that might come? What is it like to listen? Are you able to stay present and attentive? Are you able to attend to both words and the emotions?
4. *Reflect and write:*

- What was hard about this exercise?
- What did you like about it?
- Did you notice any of the tendencies discussed above: being nervous about the response or lack of response, needing more time to formulate your response, needing to be patient either while waiting for a response or while listening?
- How was your aperture awareness? Did you check in with each other about aperture levels?
- What else did you observe?

5. *Discuss.*

TALKING AND NOT TALKING

Successful communication requires knowing when to talk and when *not* to talk. For some of you, the talking part is the easy part; maybe you like confrontation, discussion, challenge— you want to just lay it all out. For some, the *not* talking part is easier; accommodation comes more easily to you, or you need more time to figure out what you think and feel before talking.

So, how do you know when to talk? And when *not* to talk? In the course of daily life, you will naturally have many moments of conflict: not liking what your partner is doing, getting your feelings hurt, et cetera. Open communication does not mean sharing difficult feelings the moment they arise. The experience of receiving negative commentary on the fly tends to make people feel anxious and cautious. For talking to be useful, you first need to create a supportive, positive atmosphere in your daily lives.

We begin by not talking. This means *not* sharing difficult feelings and issues that come up in moments when you are doing other things—cooking dinner, getting the kids ready for bed, and so forth. Instead, when your partner does something you don't like, you notice it, observe your reactions, and allow the intensity to subside and your aperture to reopen. In waiting and considering, you become more self-aware and better able to manage and learn from your reactions.

Pausing and not talking allows you to make better decisions about talking. Some of your negative reactions may be the product of fatigue, a bad mood, or a misunderstanding. Pausing allows you to understand what needs talking about and when and how to communicate to maximize understanding and support and minimize harm.

BENEFITS OF NOT TALKING
IMMEDIATELY ABOUT DIFFICULTIES

- Preserving a conflict-free environment
- Increasing your awareness
- Allowing yourself time to sort and decide what you want to talk about
- Giving yourself a chance to pick the right moment
- Allowing your closed aperture to recover

After you've given your aperture a chance to reopen, you can initiate a request for a dialogue that is negotiated and intentional. This means a talk that you have both agreed to in advance and for which each of you is ready to be open and to learn. Ideally, this request will include a few words about the topic as well as suggestions about timing. Requesting a conversation, rather than opening one unannounced, gives your partner a better chance to respond openly.

Remember that this is a *request*. It is not possible to *demand* a conversation and then have a dialogue with open apertures. Open apertures can be courted and encouraged—never commanded. The other person must feel they have a choice about whether to have the conversation and when. And the timing is important. Some conversations of moderate difficulty can be scheduled for "later tonight after the kids are in bed," while the harder ones might be best saved for "this weekend after we've taken a hike and had our favorite ice cream." Then there are conversations that have to wait until "we've finished the move," "the kids are at camp," or "you're done with your dissertation."

Here's an example of how this might work. You and your partner are cleaning the kitchen after dinner and, once again, your partner takes a phone call and disappears for the duration of the cleanup. Instead of storming into the living room with an angry confrontation right after the phone call (or, worse yet, during!), you notice that you are upset and think about whether this problem needs discussing.

Later that night, when your acute reaction has passed, you say, "I would really like to talk with you soon about our agreement to clean up the kitchen together." Bear in mind that no request for a talk about something you don't like will ever be received as completely neutral, so don't expect the first response to be open. Wait as your partner's aperture recovers enough for them to say, "Okay, let's try to talk about that this weekend."

Exercise: Not Talking

This experiment is simply about noticing and can be done for a day, a week, or longer. I suggest you start with a day, then move up to a week when you're ready, taking notes as you go. Ideally, both partners will do it at the same time, but you can do it on your own if your partner isn't ready.

Note also that for couples in a downward spiral, this exercise can be problematic. It could become an opportunity to document all your partner's mistakes, building a case against them. This will only feed your anger and discouragement. Remember, the spirit of the exercise is dialogue and the deepening of trust and connection.

1. When your partner does something you don't like, or when you become aware of something you don't like about them or the relationship,

pause and practice mindfulness. Take a moment
to notice everything you can about your negative
reaction. What emotions do you feel? What are
you thinking? What are you feeling in your body?
Notice also your reaction to "not talking" about
it. Focus on the goal of preserving a comfortable,
supportive environment.

2. Make a note. Write down the stimulus of your
    negative reaction and, if time permits, anything
    you can about your reactions.

3. Let it go and move on. (See more detailed instruc-
    tions about how to do this in Part Three.)

4. *Reflect and write.* At the end of the day, you
    should have a list of a few of these reactions—rare
    is the couple who don't have any negative reac-
    tions to each other. Some negative reactions may
    be large, others small. Go through your notes
    and add any observations you didn't have time to
    make during the day.

5. Save your list and your notes. The next exercise,
    Requesting a Dialogue, will teach you how to
    move into the "talking" part of dialogue.

Exercise: Requesting a Dialogue

This exercise is focused solely on requesting and scheduling a
dialogue. In a later exercise you will have the talk itself.

1. On separate occasions, each of you should request
    a talk. Choose a topic from your notes taken
    during the Not Talking exercise. At a moment
    when both of you are emotionally neutral, ask
    your partner for a talk about this topic. You can

suggest a time, or ask your partner to suggest a time, when you will be free of intrusions for at least a half hour.

2. When your partner asks for a talk, process it as a request. Carefully consider whether you are open to such a talk, and under what conditions. Is this something you feel comfortable talking about now? Do you need some time first to think about what you want to say? You may decide you're just not ready: "I know that's important to you, but I don't feel ready for that one yet. Let's put that off and try something else." And be sure to agree upon a time.

3. As with all the exercises, this is a chance for you to practice mindful awareness of your experience, including your aperture.

4. *Reflect and write:*

• What topic did you choose?
• What did you consider in choosing your topic?
• How did you feel in approaching your partner with this request? What was your aperture?
• What was your partner's aperture upon hearing your request?
• How did your aperture change in response to your partner's response to your request?
• If your partner declined your request, how did this affect your aperture?

Or if your partner was requesting a dialogue:

• How did you initially feel about the request? What was your aperture?

- What did you need to consider before
  responding?
- Did you agree or decline?
- How did this feel? How did it affect your aperture?

5. *Discuss.*

STARTING THE DIALOGUE

A good dialogue begins with framing. This is generally done
by the person calling for the dialogue. A good initial framing is
a brief description of the topic and what you would like to get
out of the conversation.

There are many possibilities for what we might want from
a dialogue, both in terms of the particular aspect to be discussed and the kind of conversation. Sometimes we just want
to be heard and understood. Other times we want empathy,
an apology, problem-solving, or a variety of other outcomes.
What you want may change along the way—which is fine—
but it helps to start with some attention to what you think you
want.

Keep it brief and clear. It might be something like: "I want
to talk about cleaning up the kitchen, and it's important to
me that you understand why I'm unhappy with the dishes not
being done after dinner." Recall that dialogue cannot be commanded; your initial frame is the opening of a negotiation, a
chance to discuss any differences in what you each want from
the conversation. The other person either agrees with the
frame you've suggested or modifies it. Your partner might say,
"Okay, I'm happy to talk about this, but I also want you to understand the role you play in the dishes not getting done."

The two most common mistakes with the frame are too
little and too much. Launching a conversation with too little

initial framing often results in either a lack of clarity or a lack of consensus about what is to be discussed. Both people can end up lost before they've even begun. Here's a client example of too little framing:

> **Liz:** I need to talk to you about your mother.
> **Charlie:** Look, I know my mother is an absolute disaster and I don't want to have her here either, but I just can't say no to her.
> **Liz:** Her last visit was really hard.
> **Charlie:** Right, I know. Geez, I'm sorry. Okay, from now on I'll just take the kids and go see her on my own.

Notice that the conversation is not yet framed when Charlie jumps in, first with sympathy, agreement, and a request for understanding. Then after Liz's next comment, he quickly moves to apology and problem-solving.

Here's what was happening. Though Charlie's mother is difficult, Liz had decided after his mother's recent visit that she would like to have a better relationship with her. She wanted to talk to Charlie about this new understanding. But Charlie, burdened by his own difficult relationship with his mother and eager to be understanding, jumped in with assumptions, apologies, and solutions. Though his intentions are good, Liz may give up on being understood in this conversation. She may even walk away feeling like this is another example of how Charlie just doesn't understand her. Inadequate framing led to quick assumptions, and the conversation that Liz wanted didn't happen.

At the other extreme, people try to put the whole story in the introduction. Framing a conversation is the first chance you have to slow things down and allow for reflection, awareness, and open apertures. You don't want to overwhelm your partner with your initial remarks, but rather to invite a response. Remember what you learned in the Slowing Down exercise (page 55). Trust that you will get other chances to say what you want to say. After attempting a brief frame of the conversation you want, pause to let your partner respond.

The topics you bring to your partner for discussion will very often involve something you're upset about. When you're upset, it's hard to remember that your partner will be distressed to hear that you're unhappy, especially if you're unhappy with them. Their aperture may close in self-protection. Thus, your chances of being heard increase if you can deliver this news gently. A brief framing statement followed by a pause allows them the time to ride the wave, notice any instinctive closing, and recover.

Finally, after discussing the frame, check in again on apertures. To begin the conversation you each need to be at apertures of at least 5, open enough to collaborate, learn, and stay connected. If either of you is not open enough, use the methods described in Responding to Closing Apertures (page 67). If you are not able to get open, then reschedule for another time.

Exercise: Starting a Dialogue by Framing

For this exercise, allow twenty minutes, though it may take less. You are not going to actually have the conversation but simply practice framing and beginning it.

Each of you is going to frame the conversation you proposed in Requesting a Dialogue (page 104). Thus, you will do this exercise twice, at each of the times you previously agreed on.

1. The speaker gives a simple and brief statement, a sentence or two, of what they want to talk about, including what they would like to get out of the talk.
2. Their partner responds with what they want in the conversation.
3. The two of you then negotiate what you will talk about. Here's an example:

Pete: I'd like to talk about you getting home so late in the evening. I'd like for you to understand how it affects me.

Joe: I'm fine to talk about that, and I want to include talking about what's hard for me about getting home earlier.

Pete: Yes, good.

A more complex topic may require more discussion of the frame. For example:

Pete: I'm really unhappy about being on my own with the kids in the late afternoon, and I want to talk to you about getting home earlier.

Joe: I'm not sure I can get home earlier, but I'm willing to discuss that. I'd also like to try a broader discussion of how you are doing with the kids in general. I get the feeling you're finding it difficult to be a stay-at-home dad.

Pete: Okay, that might be a longer and harder talk. Let's make sure we schedule it at a time when we can really explore all of this.

4. *Reflect and write:*

Your topic _____

Date _____

- How did you frame it?
- What was the questioning/negotiating process like?
- Were you able to be aware of apertures?
- Did either of you experience a lowering of aperture during the framing process?
- What else did you notice/learn during this exercise?

Your partner's topic _____
Date _____

- How did they frame it?
- What was the questioning/negotiating process like?
- Were you able to be aware of apertures?
- Did either of you experience a lowering of aperture during the framing process?
- What else did you notice/learn during this exercise?

ENDING THE DIALOGUE

The first aspect of a good ending is timing. But if the end point isn't necessarily when you've solved the problem or reached consensus, then how do you know when to end? In general, a good conversation about a challenging topic should last for about thirty to sixty minutes. Less than a half hour does not give you adequate time for exploration, and for most people, an hour is about as much challenging conversation as they can do well. It's hard work to have a dialogue in which you are mindful, tracking apertures, and furthering the content—all while keeping an eye on the relationship impact. These things get easier with practice, but they always require effort. After about an hour, you'll need a rest.

Ending a conversation before there is resolution can be difficult. It takes discipline, but keep in mind that most big topics will be ongoing conversations. You may need to pick it up again later.

ENDING YOUR CONVERSATION WELL

- A few minutes before ending, signal each other that it's about time to wrap up and check in to see if either of you has something to say before ending.
- Do a quick review of what you've learned.
- Review any agreements that were reached.
- Agree to continue trying to understand, and to be aware of, things that matter to your partner.
- If either of you feel you need more time with this topic, make a plan to resume the conversation.
- Appreciate each other. Take the win!

THE WEEKLY DIALOGUE

The difference between troubled relationships and relationships that are thriving is the ability to turn problems into learning. Much of this learning happens in dialogue about the relationship.

With this in mind, schedule a regular weekly dialogue

about your relationship. If talking about hard things is not a regular part of your relationship, then by definition you only do it when things get bad, or not at all! This leads to anticipatory anxiety, which means you probably avoid these talks or ask, "How bad do things need to be before we talk about them?" By making dialogue a habit, you decrease the anxiety associated with serious talks, you stop avoiding them, and you get better at them.

Once you make a practice of weekly dialogues, you may also find that sometimes there's no problem to talk about, things are going well, and you have the leisure of exploring the relationship from other angles. You might find your way back to the kind of talk that's often part of courtship, where couples spend time pleasurably learning about each other and themselves.

Taking care of your relationship means that each of you keeps an eye on what may need attention. It's a bit like taking care of your car. Most of the time you enjoy driving around. But you are also aware that it needs regular maintenance and that sometimes things get broken and need special attention.

In strong relationships, both partners stay aware of what the relationship needs. *What do we need a bit more of, a bit less of? What do we need to understand better? What injuries may need repair?*

The weekly dialogue starts with each of you saying what you want to use the time for. Avoid the temptation for either of you to "pass," leaving this job to the other person. Saying how you would suggest using the time will help each of you establish the ongoing habit of paying attention to the relationship. After each of you has proposed an agenda, you then decide together how to use the time. You may find that you agree that one topic is more important or more urgent than another. You may decide to talk about both. Or you may not agree, and you'll have to discuss a bit to decide how to proceed.

Once you've agreed on an agenda, you proceed with your chosen topic, using the aperture and dialogue skills you've learned so far.

Exercise: The Weekly Dialogue

In general, you will talk for an hour, but for the first few times you may want to start with thirty to forty-five minutes. Remember, the most important thing is to feel successful enough that you're interested in trying it again.

1. Agree on the time for your weekly dialogue, a time when you will have about an hour of privacy with no interruptions.
2. In advance, each person thinks about how to use the time. You might consult your notes about topics that came up during the week.
3. When you sit down, each person offers their suggestions. Avoid the temptation to pass.
4. Decide together how to use the time.
5. As you begin, pay attention to apertures and framing.
6. Proceed with your chosen topic, practicing the aperture and dialogue skills you've learned so far.
7. Pay attention to ending well.
8. *Reflect and write.*
9. *Discuss.* Take a few minutes to discuss your thoughts about how it went, being careful not to return to the topic. Simply share what the experience was like for you.

CHAPTER 6

Difficulties Will Arise: Strategies

In Part One you learned basic skills for staying aware of apertures, keeping them open, and reopening. This chapter gives you specific strategies for some of the most common difficulties that arise in the course of dialogue. I think of it as the tool kit.

INQUIRY

We must remind ourselves of everything we don't know, especially at moments when we hear something that feels unfair or hurtful. You can save yourself conversation derailments as well as the cumulative relationship damage that happens by pausing to inquire. Curiosity can be a life preserver; reach for it anytime you feel the seas getting choppy.

Let's look at an example. Your partner says, "I don't like you playing golf all the time." What you hear is colored by your assumptions: they don't understand your need to relax, they're jealous of your time with friends, they resent taking care of the kids, and so on. But what if you could mindfully notice your assumptions, and rather than acting on them, see your partner's comment as the start of a conversation, a dialogue? Inquiry helps the two of you move in that direction.

Let's explore three possibilities for inquiry: paraphrasing, asking questions, and encouraging your partner to say more.

Paraphrasing

Paraphrasing means saying in your own words what you think your partner is saying. Because so many tense moments for couples arise from misunderstandings, this is enormously useful. If you notice your aperture closing in response to something your partner says, a pause to paraphrase allows you to check the accuracy of your interpretation and conveys to your partner an openness and a desire to understand. You then punctuate your paraphrase with the question "Is that what you're trying to say?"

Questions

Another response when you hear something you don't like is to ask questions. Couples often make this harder than it needs to be by trying to find the *right* question. They either get stuck looking for a good question or ask an overly specific question that narrows the conversation. The best question is usually open ended. In response to "I just can't take you working all the time," an open-ended question would be: "What's hard for you about that?" But watch out for the defensive statement masquerading as a question. In this example, "Well, how do you think *I* like it!?" is technically a question, but it's not likely to get you closer to open dialogue and understanding your partner.

Say More

Then, of course, there is the most open inquiry of all: a request to "say more." This has become one of the clichés of therapy but only because it's so incredibly useful. The key to this request is your sincerity. If what you truly want is to understand better what your partner has said, and to open the dialogue, that intent and your open aperture will carry the message. The words themselves won't need to be fancy or original.

CAVEATS ABOUT INQUIRY

It's important to remember that inquiry is a request for openness. You're asking your partner to open up about their intention, needs, or concerns. When we talked about how to deal with closing apertures in the "Responding to Closing Apertures" section (page 67), I suggested that you first reassure, then inquire. The same applies here. Something simple like "I want to understand what you mean, but I'm not sure I do yet" helps the other person respond openly, instead of defensively, to your inquiry.

And, after a question or two, be sure to offer your own openness and comments. If one person keeps asking for more information, without offering something of their own, the person being questioned will feel overly exposed, like they're being interrogated instead of invited. Your partner needs to know how you're responding to them. For good dialogue, inquiry is part of the conversation, not a separate activity.

Exercise: Inquiry

This exercise is an intensive practice with specific skills. It is not meant to be a whole conversation, and it may feel awkward at times. The purpose is to focus on the skills of inquiry. Stay aware of how each step affects you, in particular your aperture. You may notice pleasure, irritation, anxiety, intensifying of various emotions, and so on.

1. Pick a topic and set a timer for twenty minutes.
2. Partner 1 will make an opening statement to which Partner 2 responds with a paraphrase, question, or invitation to say more.
3. Partner 1 responds briefly, then offers an inquiry of their own. Repeat until the timer goes off.
4. *Reflect and write:*

- What was this like for you—easy or hard, pleasant or unpleasant?
- How was your aperture affected by inquiring?
- How was your aperture affected by your partner inquiring?
- Other observations?

5. *Discuss.*

FIRST-RESPONSE PRIORITIES FOR INQUIRY

First responders learn that, across an infinite variety of scenarios, there are a few things to focus on first that help you function in complicated and intense situations. When your

aperture closes, there are three things for you to assess as soon
as possible, sort of like your first-response kit. These are:

- What's your motivation and your partner's moti-
  vation at this moment?
- Is there a possible misunderstanding?
- Is there a possible mistake?

Motivation Matters

There is a great deal of difference between an injury that results from a mistake or a misunderstanding and one that results from hostility. Motivation matters. In my experience,
rarely are the emotional injuries couples sustain from each
other intentional. The primary motivation is often a combination of a desire to connect and an attempt at self-protection.
Failure to make this distinction leads us to respond in ways
that are untrusting and further damage the relationship.

Couples who are trying to reverse a downward spiral must
constantly remind themselves that their partner is likely doing
their best to preserve a caring connection. You must maintain
awareness of your own negative assumptions and be willing to
question them.

Sensing motivation, like sensing aperture, is something we
are well equipped to do. With mindful attention, we can learn
to tell the difference between a moment when our partner is
trying to hurt us and when they are well intentioned but something has gone wrong. When apertures close, though, our ability to read motivations suffers. Sometimes we need to ask.

Even in loving relationships, when apertures close, self-
protection can turn into aggression. Is this a moment of open
aperture for your partner? Are they making a genuine attempt
at connection and dialogue? If you find that your partner's

aperture is closed, or they seem intent on winning or getting a dig in, try to address motivation and feelings directly, rather than taking up the fight. When apertures are closed, when motivations are not loving, continuing with the content is likely to make things worse. You'll need to reopen before you can proceed.

MIRROR NEURONS AND EMPATHY

Mirror neurons are part of a fascinating system that provides us with information about other people's experiences. Mirror neurons are neurons that fire when we make an action and also when we see someone else make that action. They send signals to the insula, the area that specializes in processing our bodily awareness. When the action is actually an emotional expression, mirror neurons trigger the activation of the insula and the amygdala so that your brain not only mimics the action (like a sad face) but also mimics internally the emotion associated with it. The result: You feel what others feel.

This is the true basis of empathy. We do not have an empathetic experience by imagining what we would feel in another's shoes—that's a different mental process. Rather, our mirror neurons create a felt experience, similar to the one we are observing, in our own bodies.[1]

Exercise: What's the Motivation?

This exercise will help you realize your ability to assess your partner's motivation and know when to pay special attention to this aspect of your interactions.

1. Choose a topic you think will be difficult and allow a half hour.

2. As you proceed with your dialogue, notice the moments when your aperture closes, a little or a lot, in response to something your partner says. When this happens, pause the conversation, then ask yourself what you sense about your partner's motivation. Then check with your partner about aperture. Ask your partner what motivated them to make the statement. Record these observations, yours and theirs:

   •   Your aperture closed in response to (brief phrase capturing the moment) _____

   •   Your sense of your partner's motivation _____

   •   Your sense of your partner's aperture (1–10) _____

   •   Your partner's sense of their aperture (1–10) _____

   •   Your partner's sense of their motivation _____

3. If apertures were closed, how did you return to open apertures? If either of your apertures is less than 5, use what you learned in Chapter 3, in the "Responding to Closing Apertures" section, to see if you can reopen. Then proceed with the conversation.

4. *Reflect and write.*

5. *Discuss.*

EXPECT MISUNDERSTANDINGS AND MISTAKES

Misunderstandings and mistakes account for a surprising number of the conflicts couples have. Learning to discover them quickly and to recover quickly and generously can empower you to turn things in the right direction, build trust, and conserve energy. Distinguishing misunderstandings and mistakes from the deeper challenges of differences and misalignment is part of how you turn downward spirals into upward spirals.

Misunderstandings

The world of communications is a bit hit or miss, and often we are lucky if we get in the ballpark. Verbal communication is, more often than not, incomplete, imprecise, and ambiguous. Misunderstandings happen all the time. Sometimes they do not cause a problem; they are either unimportant or are quickly cleared up. At other times, the untangling of misunderstandings can be more difficult.

Along with this inherent imprecision, our biases and beliefs influence our perception. We tend to see and hear what we expect. In a downward spiral, in addition to all the actual injuries and difficulties, couples end up dealing with imagined injuries and differences that arise from negative assumptions. Learning how to identify and deal with misunderstandings helps get things going in the right direction.

Let's look at an example. Tam and Frankie are relaxing over a glass of wine in the evening when the topic of their sixteen-year-old daughter comes up.

Tam: I'm concerned about Abby and this summer.

Frankie: Don't worry, I'm making plans to take her on a road trip to look at colleges. You'll have some time to yourself for a couple of weeks.

Tam: There you go again, thinking I'm the problem! "Let's get away from Tam and everything will be fine!"

Frankie: [With eye roll.] No matter how hard I try, I just can't please you. You're impossible!

At this point both apertures are closed. The conversation is derailed, probably the evening also. And they will likely dread the next attempt at this conversation. Right from the start, assumptions were made and each of them reacted based on their assumptions. Frankie, remembering a different conversation in which Tam had expressed a need for more time alone, thought she was offering this. Tam, influenced perhaps by her own concerns about her relationship with Abby, misunderstood the meaning of the suggestion and reacted negatively. Very quickly each felt misunderstood and thought the other person was being difficult.

Skillful handling of misunderstandings involves:

- Using your skills of inquiry whenever you feel uncomfortable with what your partner has said
- Staying alert to the likelihood of misunderstandings
- Blameless discovery and acceptance of misunderstandings
- Clarifying and moving on

Alternatively, with inquiry, it might go like this.

Tam: I'm concerned about Abby and this summer.

Frankie: Don't worry, I'm making plans to take her

on a road trip to look at colleges. You'll have some time to yourself for a couple of weeks.

Tam: Whoa, are you saying that I'm the problem in our difficulties with Abby? (This is the interpretive leap Tam made in the first version, without asking. Here, Tam is using inquiry with a question.)

Frankie: [Startled and a bit hurt.] What? No, I'm trying to give you a break! I'm remembering what you said the other day. That you feel you never get any time to yourself, and that you could be a better mother and a better partner if you had a break.

Tam: True, but what I meant about my concerns about Abby is that she and I are really struggling. I wanted to talk to you about that, and maybe how she and I could spend some time this summer doing something fun.

Frankie: Oh, I thought you wanted some time away from her. Then it really upset me that you thought I was blaming you.

Tam: Right. Sorry. It's been a hard time with her this year.

Exercise: Skillful Handling of Misunderstandings

1. Pick a topic that will be challenging. Allow a half hour for the conversation.
2. Set the timer and begin your dialogue. Whenever either of you feels a sense of closing down or discomfort or disagreement with the other, respond with inquiry.

3. When, in the course of inquiry, you discover that you have misunderstood each other, acknowledge the misunderstanding and clarify.
4. Be very disciplined about not assigning blame for the misunderstanding. This is your chance to be generous, both with your partner and with yourself. Misunderstandings are ubiquitous.
5. *Reflect and write.*
6. *Discuss.*

Mistakes

There will be mistakes—we forget an appointment, blurt out a petty comment, leave the sunroof open in the rain. Like misunderstandings, mistakes get handled very differently in upward spirals than in downward spirals. In an upward spiral, there will likely be inquiry; the mistake will be owned and forgiven, the damage kept to a minimum. In a downward spiral, negative assumptions will tend to color the interpretation of what happened, motivations and meanings may be misread, inquiries not made, and mistakes not owned or forgiven. Let's look at this exchange.

> **George:** I just want to say how much I appreciated the way you spoke to me last night about needing me to handle my spending differently; it was so much better than what usually happens.
> **Dorothy:** What do you mean by "what usually happens"?!

George wants to acknowledge a change for the better, as he and Dorothy are trying to change an old pattern, but he buries his appreciation with a reference to his long-standing frustration.

And Dorothy has grabbed the wrong end of this communication. She is not looking at George, which makes it harder to read his aperture (open) and motivation (friendly). She responds quickly, without reflecting, to the part of his message that is consistent with her fear that they can't improve the relationship. By doing so, she moves things backward. She discards the apple and eats the worm.

Here is the inflection point. With mindfulness and aperture awareness, Dorothy might ignore the mistake and respond to the compliment. She might be able to hold in mind the larger goal of understanding and learning, and ride out her initial hurt. She might say something like "Thanks for noticing. I have been trying to speak more gently to you. Next time, could you just leave it with appreciating my improvements and not remind me of the old problems?" George would then have a chance to understand what he had done, the backhandedness of his compliment. He might say something like "Sure, sorry to bring up the old stuff. I really do appreciate the changes you are making."

Notice Dorothy's skills involved here in turning the interaction in a helpful direction: aperture awareness, mindfulness, learning, slowing things down, riding the waves, eye contact. Then George quickly owned and repaired the mistake.

A mistake is actually an opportunity. Handled well, you can do more than simply limit the damage. Turning mistakes into moments of generosity makes you each feel more trusting and hopeful. In Chapter 7 we will talk more about how to handle mistakes.

RECOVERING FROM A DIFFICULT START

Letting your partner know you need a conversation about something difficult should be like a pleasing doorbell, a request to be let in. But sometimes you can't pull it off.

Anxiety about broaching a difficult subject can make it hard to request gently; your apertures may close before the end of the first sentence. Furthermore, the first sentence is unlikely to fully express what you want to talk about. And yet one needs a first sentence. I have worked with couples who were unable to talk at all for fear that their first utterance (or any utterance!) would be misunderstood. Starting difficult conversations is challenging. Mistakes will be made. You need a way forward when that happens.

Imagine your workplace has been going through a period of tight deadlines for a big project. You've been working much more than usual, racing against the clock, coming home late, often exhausted or irritable. Your partner tried making gentle requests and being patient and saying nothing. They're increasingly upset but also afraid that talking about it will only result in a nasty argument.

Finally, they decide to speak to you. Anxiety pounding in their head, they say, "I can't take it anymore. You're never home, and when you are, you're impossible to deal with." (More like nails on a chalkboard than a doorbell!)

The likely response that rises up in you, to the accompaniment of your own double-time heart rate, is something like "What do you mean I'm never home!? We just finished having dinner together; last weekend I took the kids to a ball game, and as for 'impossible,' I'd say I'm doing a pretty good job of keeping my cool for someone working as hard as I am for this family!"

And bingo! You've launched exactly the fight you both feared.

And yet, if you can ride the wave, and return to mindfulness, you may be able to treat your partner's comment as an *unpleasant request* for a conversation rather than the *failed beginning* of one. This is an example of giving your partner the benefit of the doubt. Instead of firing back defensively, you assume that the bad beginning is a result of the other being upset and consider that if your partner is feeling that strongly, a talk is probably long overdue and definitely needed.

If you can do this, your response might sound something like "Wow! I had no idea you were so upset about this. We should probably sit down soon and talk about it." Sensing your openness, your partner may find themselves opening too, with a comment like "Yeah, I'm really upset. I've been scared to bring it up. It would be great if we could talk about it." Disaster averted.

Exercise: Recovering from a Difficult Start

Because it's hard to stage such a moment, you'll need to be on the lookout for opportunities to practice.

1. Look for a moment when your partner introduces a topic in a way that lets you know their aperture is less than open; maybe it triggers yours to close.
2. Treat that statement as an awkward, uncomfortable request, letting you know that your partner wants a conversation. Remember to allow recovery from mistakes. Pay careful attention to your reactions. Wait for any strong emotional wave to pass, then try to steer toward a good recovery and a good beginning to the conversation—maybe in the moment, or maybe later.
3. *Reflect and write.*
4. *Discuss.*

DIFFERENT REALITIES

The frequency with which couples encounter differences in their realities approaches always. And the usual experience at that moment is anxiety and frustration. Our need for shared reality clashes with our need to be right, and we get uncomfortable. This is one of those necessary and normal "problems." Our frequent response then is to try to resolve this tension by vigorously debating who is right. Tempting as this is, I can assure you that the results will not be good. Dialogue is a mindful attempt to collaborate and learn from two different minds with different realities.

Krista Tippett wrote, "I can disagree with your opinion, it turns out, but I can't disagree with your experience. And once I have a sense of your experience, you and I are in relationship, acknowledging the complexity in each other's position, listening less guardedly. The difference in our opinions will probably remain intact, but it no longer defines what is possible between us."[2]

You're Both Right

In the movie *Annie Hall*, Alvy and Annie are each in therapy. We see each therapist ask how often they are having sex. Alvy says, "Hardly ever." Annie says, "Constantly." After a pause, they each say, "Three times a week." At first it seems they're giving totally different answers; the punch line reveals they're having the same experience, just from very different perspectives. They are both right.[3]

Impossible as it may seem at the moment of discovering different realities, you're both probably right. The best course forward will be to find a way to entertain this possibility. You're looking for a collaborative, open-aperture inquiry into the question *How could it be true that, though we have very different realities about this, we are both right?*

The other day I was meeting with a couple, and the wife tried to thank her husband for being more engaged with the family recently. He was instantly angry. When I asked him why, he said that it was her "story" that he had not been engaged. She then got discouraged as, in her view, once again, he denied her reality, rejecting her sense that his lack of engagement had been a problem.

After working to open each of their apertures, we set about trying to figure out how they could both be right. Here's what we discovered. He thought that by "unengaged" she meant that he was uninterested in his children and did not spend time with them. He cared deeply about his children, and when he was home (he traveled often for work), he prioritized being with them. He also didn't see his time away as a lack of engagement; his work travel was his way of taking care of the family financially. This felt to him like engaging.

She meant something different by "unengaged." Being the primary parent was very difficult for her. She wanted her husband to be more *engaged with her* for problem-solving and emotional support. So, there were certain *kinds* of engagement, different from what he'd had his eye on, that she needed more of.

As each felt the other listening and working with what they saw, they relaxed a bit. They began to see how they were both right. She then felt freer to acknowledge the ways that he *had* been engaged, and he was less defensive as he listened to her describe the kinds of engagement she wanted more of.

By now you may be noticing that this "both right" perspective is very like the old story about the blind men and the elephant. Depending on what part of the elephant each blind man is examining, the elephant is arguably a tree trunk, a snake, or a dagger. In the story, the blind men argue vigorously, failing to investigate how they might all be right. Yet a differ-ent meaning of "the elephant in the room"!

Exercise: Both Right, Part 1

You're going to explore how both you and your partner can be right about traits you see in yourself and each other. Allow about an hour for this exercise.

1. Each of you goes through the following list and writes down the traits you feel are yours.

Patient	Irritable	Generous	Frugal
Kind	Rigid	Spontaneous	Industrious
Anxious	Lazy	Absent-Minded	Creative
Tidy	Silly	Clumsy	Boisterous

    Exchange lists and choose one of the checked items that you feel is *not* a trait of your partner. If you find no points of disagreement, you might think of some positive trait you've tried to get your partner to cultivate, which they feel they already demonstrate.

2. Use the differences of opinion as a starting place for two twenty-minute conversations, each about a trait of one of you. Open the conversation by describing the difference. Then, after checking apertures to be sure each of you is at 5 or better, try to collaborate to see how you might both be right. Your initial experience will likely be a sense of certainty that you are right and your partner is wrong. It will feel like your two realities are in

opposition. The key to finding out how these two disparate realities can both be right is to *assume* that they are.

Start to explore more details and precision about what each of you means. Some things to consider:

- Are you each seeing different aspects of the same thing?
- Is your disagreement absolute, or is this a matter of proportions or shades of gray?
- Are you considering different time periods?
- Are you relating to different contexts?
- Are you using different vocabularies?
- Do your values cause you to interpret or weigh things differently?

3. *Reflect and write:*

- In what way did you turn out to be right?
- In what way did your partner turn out to be right?
- What did you discover that was unexpected?
- What did it feel like to do this?

4. *Discuss.*

Exercise: Both Right, Part 2

1. You will need a fairly challenging topic and about forty-five minutes to talk. If you already know of a topic you perceive differently from your partner, start with that. If not, just start with a topic you know will be difficult.

2. When you get to the part of the conversation where you have identified a point of divergence, slow down, check in about apertures, then proceed to work together to discover how it is that you both are right. (See the previous exercise for tips.)

3. *Reflect and write:*

- In what way did you turn out to be right?
- In what way did your partner turn out to be right?
- What did you discover that was unexpected?
- What did it feel like to do this?
- What did you like?
- What did you not like?

4. *Discuss.*

Grain of Truth

Recall that our brains have a bias against information that does not fit our existing theories. The naturalist Charles Darwin carried a special notebook in which he would record observations that did not fit his theories.[4] He knew the importance of questioning his assumptions and made a conscious effort to preserve the observations that didn't fit. The process of dialogue and integrating your lives as a couple often involves finding a way to value your partner's experience even, and especially, when it seems contrary to your own. Here's an example of what doesn't work:

Mary: You're so distracted lately that you don't even know what is going on with me.

Blake: Not true. I'm the most attentive husband we

know. I have no idea what you are talking about. For example?

Mary: The other day I told you that my sister's house was broken into and you didn't even answer, just walked out the door.

Blake: Are you kidding me? You brought this up as I was leaving for work, and I was late!

Mary: Yeah, but you never circled back.

Blake: Are you remembering that we did not see each other all week because the next day you left for your work trip?

Often when our partner confronts us with unwanted behavior, we shut down and go into argument mode. We ask the other to provide evidence, to give examples. Countless conversations run aground on this approach; all examples are refutable. As couples argue over each one, they tend to close down and get discouraged. The conversation soon sounds like two lawyers arguing in front of the jury.

Looking for the grain of truth means that, instead of asking your partner to defend their experience, you investigate your own experience for something that *relates* to what your partner is describing. You are *not* asking yourself to *agree* with your partner. Dialogue is not about whether you agree or disagree. You are asking yourself to let go of your defensive response and seriously consider your partner's experience.

It's a bit like working a jigsaw puzzle together. Your partner brings you a piece of their experience. *Grain of truth* means you go looking for another piece in your experience that might fit with theirs. Together, the pieces help you both understand the larger picture.

For example, let's say your partner claims that you're not interested in them anymore. Your first reaction is total disagreement: You love them and often think how lucky you are to be together. You feel offended that they could even think this. Then you slow down and start to search for some way that their experience might be valid and think about your three-month-old baby.

Voilà! Your grain of truth is that most of your time, energy, and attention is on the baby, which of course has resulted in less time, energy, and attention for your partner. This could feel to them like you aren't interested! In fact, you, too, are longing for your old, less encumbered life together. Life with the baby has left you with less time to enjoy each other.

Finding the grain of truth puts the two of you on the same team. The effectiveness of dialogue rests on the assumption that what you can discover together will always be more valuable to the relationship than anything one of you can understand alone.

Exercise: Grain of Truth

1. You will need approximately a half hour for this conversation.
2. One of you will be the "confronter," while the other is the "grain-of-truth finder." If you are the confronter, pick something your partner does that you don't like. Open the conversation with a strong, maybe even exaggerated, pronouncement about this behavior. For the sake of the exercise, do not try to be diplomatic.
3. After this opening statement, each of you notice your aperture. The responder then goes looking in their experience for the grain of truth in what the confronter said. Share this.

Note the movement of your apertures once the
grain of truth is offered. Then discuss what the
picture might be that includes what the confronter has offered and the grain of truth that the
other has found.

4. *Reflect and write.*
5. *Discuss.*

Beliefs and Hypotheses

Sometimes, as we try to relieve the gridlock of different realities, it's helpful to realize that our truths are actually hypotheses, and to treat them as such. In the process of trying to make
sense of the world, we form hypotheses—working theories—
about what might be true, based on our limited knowledge.
But because of our natural discomfort with not knowing, we
let these hypotheses harden into conclusions and beliefs. Being
an avid learner means recognizing how often we mistake our
own experience for the truth, and how often we are fooled by
an egocentric bias creating an experience of certainty where
we would be better served by curiosity and investigation.

By treating our truths as hypotheses, we become more
open to new experiences and information. Our apertures open
and we become effective learners, able to engage with our
partners in dialogue and to explore, instead of debate, when
we encounter differences.

Exercise: Beliefs Reconsidered as Hypotheses

In this exercise, you will practice identifying beliefs and assumptions and reconsidering them as hypotheses.

1. Choose one of your topics. Allow twenty minutes for the conversation.
2. When either of you notices a belief or assumption, your own or your partner's, call it out.
3. Try to restate the belief as a hypothesis.
4. For example, you might catch yourself saying something like "You don't care about how the house looks." You can then amend it to "I have this feeling that maybe you don't care about how the house looks." That subtle shift will make it easier for your partner to keep an open aperture and to follow with a consideration of the grain of truth—something like "That might be somewhat true; though I do really like things to look nice when we have company."
5. *Reflect and write.*
6. *Discuss.*

Offering to Investigate

If, after a few attempts at clarifying and exploring, you find that you are still stuck arguing about whose experience is the right one, you can pause the debate and agree to spend some time testing your hypotheses.

For example: Jose wants to talk to Liam about how to handle their daughter Millie's aggressive behavior during playdates. But Liam doesn't think Millie is being aggressive. They go back and forth a bit, each presenting evidence and making convincing arguments. When they notice they're repeating themselves and that apertures are closing, they stop. They agree to spend some time, maybe a week or two, studying the hypothesis that Millie's being too aggressive, perhaps even keeping notes as they go.

Now, if you are thinking that this can easily devolve into

each of them gathering evidence to support their own argument, well, you're right. The success of the investigation rests on the spirit of collaborative learning and dialogue. The goal is for Jose and Liam to learn about both Millie's behavior and their teamwork.

Exercise: Investigating Hypotheses

Practice with this exercise when you're stuck in an argument where you hold different views.

1. Begin by noticing where the conversation is getting stuck. Generally this is recognizable because you start going in circles, each of you reasserting your reality.
2. Agree to a period of data collection, during which you will both try to observe more closely the phenomenon in question. Set a date to discuss your findings.
3. As you investigate, *pay special attention to moments that seem to support your partner's hypothesis.* (Remember Darwin's notebook.) Take notes on your observations.

- Date of initial disagreement _____
- Partner 1's hypothesis _____
- Partner 2's hypothesis _____
- Time period for observation _____
- Date of next dialogue _____
- Observations _____

4. On the agreed-upon date, have a second dialogue
    in which you explore what you've learned from
    your observations.
5. *Reflect and write:*

*   How was your second conversation informed by
    your period of observation?
*   What worked about this experiment?
*   What did not work?
*   How would you change it next time?

6. *Discuss.*

Offering to Try to Understand

Perhaps the most important thing we want in our relationship
is to understand and be understood. When we don't understand our partner, it can be so uncomfortable that we end up
challenging or dismissing them, just to relieve the tension. Of
course, this usually causes them pain and makes things worse.

But failure to understand can become a moment of connection. When you don't understand your partner's experience, your desire to understand and your empathy for their
need to be understood can be deeply reassuring. Your relationship will benefit from a sincere effort to understand—even
when understanding remains elusive.

Consider an example. Sally has been trying for twenty-
five minutes to get James to understand why she does not
want to spend every vacation at his parents' house. What
James understands is that it's a great house, his parents are
very accommodating, and they've agreed to look after the
kids. What's not to like?

Sally *does* like his parents and the house and the help with
the kids. But sometimes she wants to have time just with her

husband and children. She wants to feel them being a family on their own. After multiple attempts to explain how she feels, James still isn't getting it. They could continue talking for another hour, both of them becoming increasingly exhausted and frustrated. Or James might get fed up and tell her she's simply not making sense.

But what if, instead, he says something like "I'm really sorry that I can't seem to understand what this means for you or how you feel, but I do get that it's really important and I'm glad you brought it up. Let's take a break. Let me think about it and maybe we can talk about it again soon. I will keep trying to understand." From time to time, he might mention that he's been thinking about it and still doesn't understand, but he continues to listen openly when she mentions it.

It might even happen that, one day, he comes to her and says, "You know that thing you've been talking about? Needing time for just us and our kids? I was noticing how nice it was this past week when we were all at the beach, and I think I'm starting to get it. The kids are different when it's just us. I pay more attention to them, and I think they like that." And then of course: big smiles and hugs from Sally.

Exercise: Offering to Try to Understand

For this exercise, you will have two conversations. Each partner will choose a topic on which you have not felt understood by the other.

1.   Spend about twenty minutes for each conversation. For best results, schedule these two conversations at different times.
2.   When you're in the role of wanting to be understood, your job is to convey your experience as

well as you can. This includes, of course, keeping track of apertures and pausing for apertures less than 5. Remember that you won't be understood if either of your apertures is too low.

3.   When you're in the role of trying to understand, your job is to make an effort to understand and make it clear that it matters to you. If in the end you do actually understand, or understand better than you did before, that's great. But most important in this exercise is that your partner feels your effort to understand.

4.   *Reflect and write.*

5.   *Discuss.*

THE ART OF INTERRUPTING

In some families, people talk in overlapping contributions. They interrupt each other frequently, and it's considered a sign of interest and connection. In other families, each speaker waits until the previous one has finished; interruption is considered rude and a sign of disrespect or inattention.[5] Either style can be successful, and when a couple's styles match, interruptions rarely cause conflict.

Beyond our families, in the larger world we generally learn that it's rude to interrupt. When I ask a client to interrupt *less*, they usually understand the request. But sometimes couples need *more* interruption.

Interrupting can be an important act of leadership. Good leadership involves each person taking care of and guiding the conversation. If one partner tends to speak for too long and the other follows the rule of "do not interrupt," both may end up feeling a lack of connection and dialogue. The listener will be overwhelmed and unable to respond. The speaker actually wants a response and doesn't realize that their way of talking makes this difficult. Even the speaker may get lost as they move from one thought to the next. Other couples have a pattern of alternating monologues. Although there may be balance with each taking their turn, this style still leads to both people feeling lost and disconnected.

Good dialogue requires not just articulation but time for processing. This can't happen if either or both of you speak too long. Neither of these patterns is good for dialogue. Changing these patterns often requires the listener to interrupt.

Interrupting is also about pausing. You don't need to be ready to speak in order to interrupt. Talking all the time does not enhance dialogue. You need time to reflect and process. An interruption might be followed quickly by a comment, but more often the interrupter will need some time to process what they've just heard and consider what they want to say before speaking.

Exercise: The Art of Interrupting

You're going to practice interrupting and being interrupted.

1. You will need a topic and about a half hour.
2. Before you begin your conversation, reflect on what you have observed so far about your dialogue style as a couple. Which of these describes your usual pattern?
   - Overlapping, interruptive style
   - Sequential style
   - Sequential monologues
   - Balanced or one of you talks more (who is the "talker"?)

3. Set a timer for twenty minutes and begin the con-
    versation. When it's your turn to speak, *don't* stop
    until your partner interrupts.
4. When you are the listener, wait for a moment
    when you would like the speaker to pause. When
    that moment arrives, interrupt immediately, ask-
    ing your partner to pause. Then take any time you
    need to reflect before speaking. Once you start,
    you are the speaker until your partner interrupts.
5. *Reflect and write.*
6. *Discuss.*

PRESENTING THE PROBLEM INSTEAD OF THE SOLUTION

Mary and Joe live in a wonderful house that they love. As the
kids get older, Mary hears from the neighbors that the local
public schools aren't great. After some research, she decides
that they should put the kids in private school. Knowing that
Joe is very cautious with their finances, she chooses her moment carefully, asks to talk, and then presents him with the
evidence she's gathered, followed by her conclusion that they
clearly will have to put the kids in private school.

Rather than exclaiming what a clever wife he has, Joe bris-
tles, then pushes back. As the disagreement escalates, Mary
feels her efforts and insights are unappreciated. What happened? Mary, an excellent problem solver, presented Joe with
her preferred solution rather than coming to him with the
problem.

Multiple influences incline us toward solo problem-
solving. Foremost is speed and efficiency. Consensus can be
laborious. Finding the time and energy to collaborate can be
hard. And, for some, the interdependence of being a couple is

uncomfortable and raises anxieties; self-sufficiency sometimes feels safer.

Minimizing conflict plays a role here too. When it comes to problem-solving, the natural differences in values, priorities, and preferences can lead to conflict. Prior to learning the skills of dialogue, couples often anticipate these differences and prepare the arguments for their solution like a good lawyer going to court. This approach is practically guaranteed to lead to argument instead of collaboration.

Most people want to participate rather than have their partner solve the problem for them. Imagine how differently the conversation might go if Mary, instead of presenting Joe with the solution, presents him with the problem. She might open with "I'm concerned about the quality of the local schools, and I think we need to talk about it." Together they might consider a few possible solutions: paying for tutors, moving to another school district, private school.

In addition to encouraging collaboration instead of conflict, presenting the problem rather than the solution often produces more possible solutions than either would think of alone. Also, hard choices are easier to make when both partners have been involved in problem-solving from the start. Even more important is the impact on the relationship. Being asked to participate conveys trust, respect, openness, and connection. The implicit message in asking your partner to help you solve a problem is *I value you, and I want your ideas and opinions. I want the outcome to be influenced by your preferences. I want connection with you.*

Exercise: Presenting the Problem Instead of the Solution

Each partner should come prepared with a problem they've

been trying to solve. It might be something that affects the couple, the whole family, or something that, though not central to your partner's concerns, will affect them in some way. Do this exercise twice so that you each get to practice both roles.

1. Dialogue for about twenty minutes each time.
2. Begin your dialogue by presenting the problem, using what you learned in the Starting a Dialogue by Framing exercise (page 108). As you discuss, pay attention to any tendency that emerges on either side to argue for a particular solution. Keep the conversation going in the direction of open exploration by following these guidelines:

- Pay attention to apertures.
- Stop for apertures less than 5.
- Slow down.
- Maintain a balance.
- Notice any discomfort with "not knowing," and try to hang out with it, observing mindfully.
- Remember that the most important outcome is the effect on the relationship.

3. *Reflect and write:*

- What was challenging for you?
- What did you learn?

4. *Discuss.*

OWNING YOUR PARTNER'S AGENDA

Psychotherapist Irvin D. Yalom writes, "To love means to be actively concerned for the life and the growth of another."[6] One reason that conversations, and relationships, can get stuck is that partners are not valuing and protecting each other's needs, wants, and priorities. In good dialogue, each of you owns and defends what matters to *you*, as well as what matters to *your partner*. Putting the relationship first means that you *both* aim to understand as much as possible what *each* person wants and to find solutions that protect and enhance the relationship.

This is quite different from each person advocating for their own needs and negotiating a compromise. Couples often assume that quid pro quo is the goal, but this is still a negotiation of adversaries where the shared goal of strengthening the relationship is lost.

For example, Sue and Jerry are talking about the summer, looping through a familiar cycle of arguing. Sue hasn't seen her sister in over a year and wants to spend a week with her. Jerry has a very demanding job, and he's concerned that he won't be able to handle the three small children on his own. Each one is stating and restating their concerns, as if the goal is simply to overpower or outlast the other side. The underlying assumption is that only one person will get what they want.

It's a very different conversation when each of them owns the other's agenda. Jerry then considers how important it is to Sue to see her sister, and Sue thinks about how much she doesn't want Jerry to be overwhelmed while she's gone. They hold in mind that if their partner feels too deprived or resentful, the relationship will suffer, and each of them will lose.

When they identify as a team, searching for a way for Sue to see her sister without stranding Jerry, options emerge that were unavailable when they were acting as adversaries. Sue says she could go during July, when all three kids are in summer camp. Jerry remembers that his mom has been wanting to make a trip to see the kids, and that maybe she could come help while Sue is gone. One of their kids is the same age as one of Sue's sister's kids; maybe Sue would take that child with her. Maybe Sue's sister could come to them. All of these possibilities emerge from their mutual investment in a solution that meets each of their needs.

Exercise: Owning Your Partner's Agenda

For this exercise, you will need a problem to solve that you have disagreements about. (Most couples have a few of these!)

1. Allow about an hour.
2. Before beginning your conversation, each of you should make a quick list of your ideas for solving the problem. Put this list aside for later.
3. Dialogue for a half hour. In the first phase of this dialogue, listen and try to understand each other's requests, preferences, and needs. After you've heard from your partner, paraphrase what you think they want. Continue this process until each of you feels that your partner understands what's important to you.
4. Work together to create solutions that address what you both want. You might not find the perfect solution, but the goal here is for your partner to feel that you are championing their needs as much as your own. Keep your attention on apertures, collaboration, and putting the relationship first.
5. *Reflect and write:*

- Make a list of the solutions that emerged from your dialogue.
- Review your first list of solutions.
- What solutions emerged in the course of the dialogue that you hadn't thought of alone?
- What were the challenges for you in holding and championing both your needs and those of your partner?
- What were the pleasures in doing this?
- Do you feel that this dialogue enhanced the relationship? If so, in what way? If not, why not?

6. *Discuss.*

TIME-OUT AND DISTANCE

Starting or continuing a conversation when either partner's aperture is closed is likely to harm the relationship. It's the equivalent of running a stop sign. We've talked about how to respond to closing apertures: pause, reopen, and resume the conversation (page 67). But sometimes this is not possible. Sometimes you or your partner may not be able to reopen, and in these cases you may need to discontinue the conversation.

When you realize that either of you cannot reopen, call for a time-out. Under no circumstances should you say, "We have to stop now because your aperture is closed." This will likely not go well; it can feel like you're blaming your partner, who then will become defensive. The best way to call a time-out is to simply say that you don't feel it's a good idea to continue right now, adding that you are happy to revisit the conversation another time. You can schedule that in the moment or wait until later. At this point, the two of you should move to different rooms to avoid the temptation to resume.

Time-outs are essential, but they're also very difficult for some people. Some people feel a need to find a solution *right now*; others may feel abandoned by the stop. Often one partner will want to stop and the other won't. Handle this as gently as possible. Helping each other avoid the damage that can happen by talking with closed apertures is an aspect of good leadership, teamwork, and putting the relationship first.

We often think of moving away from a loved one as an unloving act, a blow to the relationship. But the right use of distance optimizes love and intimacy, while minimizing harm to each person and the relationship. In a well-functioning relationship, the partners are constantly modulating closeness and distance. (For people with special sensitivities to abandonment, learning to be lovingly apart can be challenging but also very healing. If this is the case for you or your partner, you may want to explore counseling to support your efforts.)

Exercise: Time-Out

1. This is likely to be a challenging exercise. When either of you experiences an aperture below 5 from which you cannot recover, both of you are likely to feel pretty uncomfortable. This is what aperture awareness and the skills related to open apertures are designed to avoid. And yet it will happen, especially with difficult topics. For some couples, this is a common occurrence; for others, it's rare. Select a difficult topic and set your timer for a half hour.

2. Keep track of apertures. If either person's aperture falls below 5, and the two of you cannot succeed in opening up again, call a time-out.

3. Call the time-out with no attribution of blame.

4. If you are asking for the time-out, offer to reopen the discussion at a later time. Then make sure that you follow up.

5. If your partner is asking for the time-out, remember that for challenging conversations to be successful, you both need to feel ready to proceed.

6. Do not reengage until both of you have returned to apertures of 5 or above.

7. *Reflect and write.* Each time you use this strategy, take a few notes about what you observed:

- Who called the time-out?
- Is one of you more likely to call the time-out than the other?
- How do you feel when your partner calls a time-out?
- How do you feel when you call a time-out?
- What's difficult about doing this?

8. *Discuss.* Make sure that you wait until apertures are fully open again and you both feel ready to consider how it worked. You may want to discuss each time one of you calls a time-out or wait until you have had a few time-outs to discuss all your observations.

CHAPTER 7

Repair

Inevitably, people in relationships hurt each other. We can't dance closely without sometimes stepping on toes. Fortunately, the strength of a relationship does not depend upon avoiding hurt, but on how well we recover together.

Attachment research tells us that secure bonds form where there is connection, disruption of the connection, and then a satisfying repair and reconnection.[1] In this way, we learn to trust that reconnection after disruption is possible, we don't have to be perfect to be loved, and conflict and separation are survivable. Relationships in which partners feel safe to explore, take risks, and sometimes screw up are stronger than those in which partners feel they have to be perfect. Knowing that repair is possible also makes it easier to identify and acknowledge our mistakes and less likely that we will minimize each other's injuries. Skillful repair of difficulties and injury builds trust in yourself, your partner, and your relationship.

Frans de Waal, who spent his career studying social

behavior in primates, found that chimpanzees go through a reconciliation process after conflict. "This kind of behavior," he wrote, "is not at all limited to primates: hundreds of reports find it in other social mammals and in birds, so much so that if anyone were to claim that a given species doesn't make up after fights we'd be baffled." He goes on to describe the importance of repair and the emotional agility it requires:

> Conflict resolution is part and parcel of social life. The emotions involved are hard to pinpoint, but a minimum requirement is that anger and fear—the typical emotions during a confrontation—are toned down in order to permit a more positive attitude. This reversal is rather counterintuitive. Someone who has just lost a fight with a dominant attacker now needs to pluck up the courage to approach him or her for a friendly reunion. Meanwhile the aggressor must suddenly drop the enmity, which is illogical. But many animals undergo these emotional changes remarkably rapidly, as if a control in their mind were turned from hostile to friendly.[2]

In other words, we have evidence that the need for repair is so strong that we may be willing to calm down, be courageous, and drop our grievances.

Human couples, like other social animals, feel distress when their connection is disrupted. One characteristic of a well-functioning couple is the ability to experience and respond to this distress. Tronick wrote, "In (resilient) dyads, the negative affect associated with disrupted attunement is a motivational spur toward repair and the restoration of coordination."[3]

When I'm teaching and I raise the issue of apologies, a groan goes through the room. In working with couples, I sometimes find that apologies are not being offered because they are defined as admissions of guilt. When things go wrong, people pull back into adversarial assumptions, focusing on who is to blame, who is wrong, who is guilty.

Look at any news story and you'll see how often establishing blame is treated as the solution to the various injuries and disruptions of social relationships. Our culture is litigious and adversarial. This understanding of apology as an admission of guilt gets in the way of repair.

"What flower says you're sorry without admitting wrongdoing?"

Credit: Mike Twohy, The New Yorker Collection / The Cartoon Bank

In the disruption and injury that happens in couples, finding who's guilty is the least important part. In fact, it's usually not necessary at all. Yes, really! Couples do recover and strengthen the relationship without establishing blame.

THE THREE ASPECTS OF REPAIR

When injury occurs, three aspects of the relationship may need repair: the empathetic connection, shared reality, and agreements and expectations.

Aspect 1: Repair of the Empathetic Connection

Repair of the empathetic connection is the most important, the first, and usually the easiest. Empathetic connection defines our relationship as allies instead of adversaries. We count on our partners to feel our distress and be invested in our happiness. If we feel injured, we question this empathetic connection, sometimes subtly or unconsciously, sometimes explicitly. This is especially true in a downward cycle. After an injury, we need to first be reassured that our partner cares about our distress and does not wish us harm. Remember, motivation matters.

Ideally, "I'm sorry" comes as soon as you realize that your partner is injured. This is where the distinction between "I'm sorry you feel hurt" and "I'm sorry I screwed up" comes in. This "I'm sorry" means: "It matters to me that you have been injured or upset. I care about you, and when you feel bad, I care about that."

For example, imagine your partner calls you at 8:45 a.m. as you're pulling into the parking lot at work. He's furious.

> "Matt's still here and needs a ride to school. I'm supposed to be at the dentist in ten minutes."
>
> "You were supposed to take him. I told you I had to go in early."
>
> "That's not what we agreed last night."
>
> "But this morning, I told you things had changed. I can't miss this meeting."

"Great! So, now I have to reschedule my dentist. Do you know how hard that is?!"

"Look, I'm really sorry that this happened. There's no way I can help at this point. I think you'll have to drive him. I'm really sorry this is going to mess up your morning."

Note the expression of concern and regret without establishing whose fault it is. We do not have to feel that we have erred in order to be distressed that our partner is in pain.

Sorting out issues of responsibility can be quite difficult, requiring honesty, openness, humility, and generosity from both participants. At the moment of injury, it's unlikely that either of you is open enough to have the best version of the discussion. For this reason, separating the repair of empathy from the examination of responsibility is helpful, even necessary. This immediate reassurance to your partner that you really do care will keep things from getting worse and set the stage for the more complicated repair later.

There's a tricky aspect to this. When we feel injured by our partner, our emotional reality often is that our hurt feelings are a result of wrongdoing on their part. In those wonderful moments when they instantly agree that they screwed up, all is well. But very often the issue of culpability is ambiguous.

Many people feel that "I'm sorry you feel hurt" instead of "I'm sorry I hurt you" is a cop-out, a ducking of responsibility. And it can be. But defining it this way emphasizes blame and makes repair harder.

If you consistently offer caring as a beginning to repair instead of a way of avoiding responsibility, your partner will come to trust that "I'm sorry you got hurt" is not a way of denying responsibility but a way to open the door to the more difficult repair of shared reality, responsibility, and agreements.

Learn to link "I'm sorry you got hurt" to "Let's talk about it later." And of course be sure to follow through.

THE ALTERNATIVE TO KEEPING SCORE

While accountability is extremely important, couples often decrease trust rather than build it by vigilantly policing each other. We do not help each other offer our best when we overemphasize criticism and keeping score. For effective repair that builds trust, change your priorities from keeping score and being self-protective to creating openness, exploration, and acceptance. In an atmosphere where both mistakes and forgiveness are expected, it becomes easier to offer "I'm sorry."

Aspect 2: Repair of Shared Reality

The most common mistake couples make when there is injury is to go immediately to the discussion of what happened and whose fault it is. When you're hurt, it can feel urgent and necessary to get your partner to agree with you about what happened, including and especially their responsibility in it. But going immediately to this discussion is a mistake. This conversation will often be extremely difficult, and it's essential that you come to it with open apertures. Empathetic repair helps you do this.

Aspect 2 is a dialogue about what each of you experienced. The second thing that needs repair when there is injury is a sense of shared reality. Recall that we need to feel there's agreement about reality in order to feel safe and sane. Between couples, even a small disruption of shared reality can cause distress, as in the miscommunication about who was to take Matt to school.

The consensus we want is that our experience is true, but experience is very subjective and memory very fallible. It's important to hear each other's reality, with no attempt to decide who is right or wrong, or even to agree or disagree. The goal is to articulate your experience and hear about your partner's.

By working with this expanded understanding of how a shared world is built, it becomes possible to see how your two different experiences resulted in conflict and injury. You can go beyond "agreeing to disagree."

Aspect 2 will help you clarify whether the injury resulted from a misunderstanding, a mistake, or an intent to injure. As discussed on page 121, "Misunderstandings," discovering that injury resulted from misunderstanding is actually very good news and accepting misunderstandings as inevitable without trying to assign blame can be a loving way out of difficulty.

Sometimes in your discussion of what happened you will find that one or both of you has made mistakes. When you discover you've made a mistake, apology is called for. Many of us try too hard to be perfect and punish ourselves, or our partners, when we are not. This results in us failing to recognize our own mistakes, failing to offer repair and apology, and failing to be generous with forgiveness.

Mistakes will happen. By owning mistakes, asking forgiveness, and granting forgiveness, you increase safety and trust. Expect that you both will make many mistakes and view each of them as an opportunity for the repair that strengthens your relationship.

Many mistakes result from strong emotions and closed apertures—partners say things they don't really mean when they're hurt or angry. Other times, though, the intent to harm or unwillingness to act lovingly is more than a momentary problem. If you find this is the case, you'll need to reassess your commitment to the relationship and perhaps consult a therapist. Fear of discovering this kind of deeper problem often keeps couples from really delving into Aspect 2.

Not all successful repairs immediately result in a return to harmony. Keep in mind that repairs can strengthen the relationship without necessarily leaving everyone feeling jolly.

An attempt to repair shared reality sets the stage, though is not absolutely necessary, for Aspect 3.

Exercise: Apology for Mistakes

Because we inevitably make many mistakes, generally every day, with our partner, it will be easy for you to practice handling this skillfully. Don't wait until you make a big mistake; this would be a hard place to start. Instead, be on the alert for all the little things—like you forgot to mention that you won't be home for dinner, you parked your car in a way that made it hard for your partner to get in the driveway, or you left your wet towel on the floor.

1. Be on the lookout for your small mistakes.
2. As soon as you recognize one, go to your partner with an apology.
3. Think about what you may need to do to avoid future mishaps.
4. Be generous with self-compassion and self-forgiveness.
5. When your partner makes a mistake, be generous with compassion and forgiveness. Humility and

self-compassion about your own mistakes will
help you do this.

6. *Reflect and write:* What is hard for you about
    apologizing? What's hard about accepting an
    apology?
7. *Discuss.*

Aspect 3: Repair of Agreements and Expectations

In the third step, you consider: Did this injury happen because
we don't agree about how we should treat each other? If you
conclude that the cause of the injury was a mistake, misunderstanding, or lack of motivation, then you most likely have a
shared idea about what *should have happened* in the situation.
In that case, this step amounts to quick reaffirmation of agreements. For example, you agree that you should not yell at each
other in front of the kids, but someone lost their temper and
broke that agreement.

But sometimes it turns out that you do not agree on what
should have happened. Maybe you don't have an agreement, or
you may discover that a previous agreement no longer works
for one or both of you and needs revisiting. You scheduled a
business trip without discussing it in advance. Perhaps in the
past you agreed to discuss all business travel with each other
before making plans, but now one of you is finding this too
cumbersome. In this case, you need to reopen the discussion
of what agreement is best for the relationship.

To summarize: In a good repair process, couples work together to reaffirm their caring for each other (empathetic repair), understand what happened (shared reality repair), and
clarify agreements (repair of agreements and expectations).
A successful repair process begins with injury but results in
deeper understanding of each other and a strengthening of
trust and connection.

REPAIRING MAJOR DAMAGE

Repairs, like injuries, come in different sizes. The previous section describes repair for a relatively simple, onetime injury. But suppose the injury is large, like an affair? Or repeated, as with a period of substance abuse? In these cases, the damage is significant and lasting. You will need many conversations and many repetitions of each part of the repair: "I do care about you"; "I'm sorry you were hurt"; "I agree that I behaved in a destructive way"; "I agree that I should not do this in the future."

This kind of healing is often measured in years. The amount of time and effort it will take is likely to strain the patience of both parties. Part of repair after major injury is the willingness and ability to hang in there. And, paradoxically and frustratingly, the more impatient you are, the longer it will likely take.

In these situations, one or both partners may wonder whether the relationship can survive. *Is repair even possible? Will we be able to love again, trust again? How long will the repair take, and is it worth the effort?* Answering these questions may take time, and your answers may change in different phases of recovery as you sort through feelings of betrayal, disappointment, anger, failure, guilt, and fatigue.

It can be very hard during this process to know whether things are getting better. After major injury, you are in a serious downward spiral. You may have to work hard, and for a long time, before things start to shift. The conversations required for this kind of recovery are usually risky. You will inevitably stir up painful experiences, possibly reinjuring each other. Emotions will be intense, sometimes including depression, anxiety, and symptoms of post-traumatic stress disorder (PTSD).

In situations where one partner was clearly the offender, there is the added complication of shame for the offender and victimization for the other partner. These are normal reactions, but if mishandled, they can intensify the damage. Part of the harmful power of these reactions is in the illusion that the injuries can be resolved through punishment, either of oneself or of one's partner. Punishments are extensions of pain masquerading as resolution. You will need to spend time understanding these reactions and getting beyond them in order to grieve, forgive, and heal.

Couples do manage to repair major injuries, but only with sufficient motivation, patience, time, and, often, professional help. Think of it as you would a physical injury. When we scrape a knee, cut a finger, or twist an ankle, we know how to handle these on our own; we trust that our bodies will generally heal easily and quickly. But when we break a bone or have malfunction in a major organ, we need the special skills of experts and extended time for healing. The more serious the injury and difficult the recovery, the more likely we'll need someone to guide us, monitor our progress, and reassure us. The idea of working with a therapist may be foreign and uncomfortable, yet I encourage couples to consider it, especially those with major damage to repair. After all, you wouldn't try to set your own broken leg!

Though not for the faint of heart, couples who make it through this journey often emerge with valuable learning and a stronger relationship. More than once couples have said to me that though they never would have chosen to go through such an agonizing period, they're enormously grateful for what they gained.

THE CHALLENGES OF MAJOR REPAIR

- Assessment of the injuries
- Understanding the tasks of the several phases of a major repair
- Sustaining your motivation through the difficult and lengthy process
- Avoiding further damage as you work to repair
- Knowing how to read the signs of progress
- Knowing when to get professional help

PART THREE

Mindfulness and Internal Skills

I'm not afraid of storms, for I'm learning how to sail my ship.

—Louisa May Alcott[1]

CHAPTER 8

Mindful Awareness and Emotions

Our emotions have a life of their own. Creatures of caprice and whimsy, they are sometimes delightful, sometimes painful. They both bark and bite, sometimes sting and sometimes sing. Like guests that arrive and depart without notice, they sometimes leave behind a mess, sometimes flowers.

Up to now, the focus has been on what happens *between* the two of you. But as you have attempted new behaviors, you probably have become aware that your *internal* reactions—your thoughts and emotions—facilitated or hampered your effectiveness. Producing the external behaviors that lead to good and great relationships requires competency in various feats of self-management and acrobatics of attention. In this chapter, you're going to learn about mindfulness and the skillful handling of emotions—the basis for open apertures, productive dialogue, and loving relationships. You will have a chance to practice experiencing your emotions without letting them run the show. While we do not have absolute *control* over our thoughts, feelings, and impulses, mindfulness gives us the ability to handle them in ways that are good for our relationship.

Emotional experience can be uncomfortable, sometimes extremely uncomfortable. If, as children, we are in the company of adults who are skillful at tolerating and regulating intense emotions, we acquire implicit knowledge of how to do this and how to learn from our awareness. Lacking this experience, we do the best we can, which may involve figuring out how to *not* feel our emotions, waiting helplessly for them to subside, or possibly learning that certain behaviors, like getting angry and yelling, distract us and relieve our discomfort. But these strategies limit our ability to learn and connect. Fortunately, it's never too late to learn better strategies. The special magic of intimate, committed relationships is that they provide the motivation for this demanding learning, resulting in the acquisition of the internal skills that help us to live and love powerfully, and with integrity.

WHAT ARE EMOTIONS?

We register information about each moment's complex fabric of meanings through sensing internally in our bodies, a process known as interoception. Basically, sensations from inside our bodies (the often-subtle sensations in our internal organs) travel to the limbic system, the insula, and then to our prefrontal cortex. This area also receives a vast array of other information and memories that get collated to provide us with the complex experiences we know as emotions. We then may become consciously aware that we are having a "feeling."[1]

Every "feeling" has three components—emotional, physical, and mental—but we often are more aware of just one. On the way to the dentist, one person feels anxious (emotional), another has a queasy stomach (physical), and a third is thinking, *I wish I didn't have to do this* (mental). We're going to refer to emotional experience, but bear in mind that it may manifest in a variety of ways. The goal of this chapter is to explore what emotions are and how we can become more mindfully aware of them.

We used to think that emotions were superfluous annoyances. Now, we understand that emotions are central to intelligent processing. They are one of our many sources of information about the world and ourselves. Antonio Damasio and other neuroscientists have studied the neural systems underlying emotion, decision-making, memory, language, and consciousness. They've found that emotions play a central role in our decision-making processes, and people who consider how they feel about their choices tend to make better decisions.[2]

THE IMPORTANCE OF "GUT" REACTIONS

Antonio Damasio formulated the Somatic Marker Hypothesis, which proposes that when confronted with decisions, our first move, usually unconsciously, is to run it by our "gut reaction." This lets us know how we "feel" about the options—which are acceptable and which are not. The choices our *conscious* mind then considers are those that have already passed the first screening of our emotional system. This hypothesis was formed around Damasio's study of people with particular brain lesions. If their lesions impair their ability to know how they feel about things, they are unable to take action. Even simple things like getting on an elevator or taking the stairs stop them in their tracks; they don't have the necessary emotional information to make choices.[3]

THE POWER OF TAKING RESPONSIBILITY

We may have uncomfortable emotional reactions to a great variety of things: delays in traffic, the death of a pet, a bad review at work, or even another sock eaten by the dryer! But we especially have uncomfortable emotional reactions to some of the things our partners do.

If your partner does something that is not good for you, it's important to be able to talk to them about it, ask them to be responsible for their actions, and possibly change their behavior. But the process of dealing with the emotional *discomfort* generated by their behavior, including recovering, is your responsibility. This distinction can be difficult to grasp.

The idea that one cannot feel better unless or until their partner does something to make them feel better is a leftover from our infant selves. As infants, we needed a lot of help to manage the overwhelming experiences of hunger, cold, thirst, and a variety of other discomforts. As adults, it's possible to learn internal skills for dealing with discomfort. In order for this learning to happen, we must hold ourselves responsible for recovery and resilience when we are upset.

Mindfulness, Containment, and Response Flexibility

Mindful awareness is the key to self-management. Without mindfulness, your fast-track processing of a stressful situation produces a reaction before you're even aware of what is happening. Many of our interactions with our partners happen in this way; we react in habitual ways with no chance to reflect. The external reaction momentarily relieves tension and decreases discomfort, sometimes referred to as "letting off steam." This is one way to rid yourself of this troublesome experience.

EMOTIONAL STIMULUS → REFLEXIVE RESPONSE

Figure 6: Fast-Track Reaction

Another solution is to shut down your awareness of the feeling. This doesn't make it go away; your body still experiences the stress of it from the effects of the surge of cortisol and adrenaline. But you have managed to move it out of conscious awareness—a sort of self-anesthesia.

Neither of these strategies does much for your learning.

The third alternative is that you inhibit the behavioral reaction, but stay aware of your uncomfortable experience. This is sometimes called *containment.* Containment means that instead of trying to get rid of the uncomfortable internal reaction, you *hold* it—much like a bowl might contain soup. Now, instead of ignoring or getting rid of your experience, you have a chance to study it. Like the soup, when well digested these experiences nurture our growth. You observe and learn. You investigate. You also learn how to do this interesting and useful thing called *mindful awareness.*

Furthermore, as you sit with your experience without reacting, your slow-track cortical processing has a chance to catch up—to consider in more detail how external events are related to your internal experience and what are the various options for behavioral *response.* You gain what Dan Siegel, UCLA psychiatrist, calls "response flexibility." "Mindfulness,"

Siegel writes in *The Mindful Brain*, "creates a space between impulse and action that allows us to be more flexible in our responses."[4]

EMOTIONAL STIMULUS → CONTAINMENT, MINDFULNESS → RESPONSE FLEXIBILITY

Figure 7: Response Flexibility

As you practice this mindful containment and awareness, your brain becomes more active and able to modulate emotional intensity. You learn to quiet your internal reactions. You teach yourself to experience difficulties with less distress.

Learning this, however, takes some practice. In the beginning it may be quite uncomfortable. It might go something like this: Your partner says, "You left the garage door open again. I'm sick of you spacing out about this!"

You notice that you are about to respond: *Are you kidding me?! You do that all the time!* But you remember to pause and not speak reactively. You immediately notice that this is hard. Everything in you wants to return fire. The effort not to speak is considerable. You notice that you are holding your breath. You exhale and draw in a deep breath. You feel slightly better but are still quite upset. You continue noticing your breath. You are practically panting with the effort, maybe even sweating. This is hard.

The first time you try this, that might be it. Your partner might walk away, wondering why you did not respond. Or maybe you just mumble something like "Uh, okay." By delaying your reaction, you have kept yourself from escalating conflict when both your apertures were closed. Or maybe, after your effort to contain and observe, you do blurt out, "Are you kidding me?! You do that all the time!" But even if you do, you have had a few moments of mindfulness, of suspending reaction in order to observe whatever you can about what is going on. That's progress!

You have already practiced containment with mindfulness in the exercises Ride the Waves (page 63) and Not Talking (page 103). Now would be a good time to repeat these exercises. You've probably learned a lot since you first did them. Notice how they feel the same or different this time.

Verbalizing Emotion

Observation and awareness are the prerequisites for the third key to skillful internal self-management: verbalizing emotional experience. We need to be able to put emotions into words for two reasons. The most obvious of these is that communicating what we're feeling creates understanding and connection with our partner.

Verbalizing also helps us connect to and understand ourselves. Research suggests that we don't really know what we are feeling until we put it into words.[5] Language integrates, organizes, and regulates the brain.[6] Words do much of the work of connecting the various parts of the brain so that thoughts, emotions, physical sensations, and memories get integrated into a whole experience that is then available to inform our next understanding or behavior. Containment of uncomfortable emotions helps us to be mindfully aware of them; mindful awareness in turn helps us talk about them; talking enhances awareness.

CONTAINMENT ⟷ AWARENESS ⟷ VERBALIZATION

Figure 8: The Interrelatedness of Containment, Awareness, and Verbalizing

One reason people hesitate to talk about uncomfortable

emotions is that verbalizing emotions can intensify emotional experience. However, research shows that if we can say a *few words* that describe our experience, especially words that are concrete or metaphoric, the intensity of the experience is *diminished*. However, if we speak at length, we will *amplify* the experience.[7] Thus, when you decide to continue beyond your few words of description, be aware that you'll need to manage this intensification. Amplifying an emotional experience can help you understand it better, but beyond a certain point it can be counterproductive. Verbalizing emotions skillfully is discussed in the next chapter.

Exercise: Verbalizing Emotions Briefly

In this exercise, each of you is going to experiment with saying a few words about an emotional experience. You can both do this exercise in the same session or at different times.

1. You will need about fifteen minutes for each of you (including reflection and writing) and a timer.
2. Take a few minutes to choose an emotional experience you would like to verbalize. This should be something that was a strong experience for you at the time, either positive or negative. Recent experiences are more likely to be fresh, but it could be something in the distant past. And it could be something you feel or have felt in response to your partner, but it doesn't have to be.
3. Your partner is going to set the timer for a minute. You don't have to use the whole minute, but you must stop speaking when the minute is up.
4. You are to speak as clearly and accurately as you can about the feelings you had on this occasion.

Avoid the temptation to tell the whole story of the events. The story you are telling is of your emotional experience.

5. Your partner is to listen attentively, but without responding or helping.

6. *Reflect and write:*

- What was this like for you?
- Did a minute feel short or long, or just right?
- What did you feel at the end of the minute?

7. *Partner reflect and write:*

- What was it like to listen?

8. *Discuss.*

Exercise: Verbalizing Emotions at Length

In this exercise, each of you is going to experiment with a lengthy description of an emotional experience. Do these two sessions at different times. Be aware that verbalizing at length is likely to amplify an emotional experience. Keep this in mind in terms of decisions about when to do this and what to choose to express. The goal here is learning, not catharsis.

1. You will need about twenty-five minutes for each of you (including reflection and writing) and a timer.

2. Take a few minutes to choose an emotional experience you would like to verbalize. This should be something that was a strong experience for you at the time, either positive or negative.

Recent experiences are more likely to be fresh, but it could be something in the distant past. And it could be something you feel or have felt in response to your partner, but it doesn't have to be.

3. Your partner is going to set the timer for five minutes. You are going to try to speak for the whole time, saying as much as you can capture about this experience. Stop when the five minutes are up.

4. You are to speak as clearly and accurately as you can about the feelings you had on this occasion. You can include details of what happened if that helps you tell of your emotional experience.

5. Your partner is to listen attentively, but without responding or helping.

6. *Reflect and write:*

- What was this like for you?
- Did five minutes feel short or long, or just right?
- What did you feel at the end of the five minutes?
- How was five minutes of verbalizing different from one minute?

7. *Partner reflect and write:*

- What was it like to listen?
- How was five minutes of listening different from one minute?

8. *Discuss.*

Emotional Contagion

Another aspect of containment has to do with handling

emotional contagion. Even when we're not intentionally expressing them, emotions are contagious. And the closer we are to others, the more time we spend with them, the more likely it is that they feel our emotions and are affected by them, sometimes "catching" them.

On the one hand, this ability to sense our partner's emotions forms the basis for empathy and intimacy, and when the emotions are pleasant, it can be delightful. On the other hand, there are times when this ability needs to be managed to maximize understanding and closeness, while minimizing discomfort and disruption. Awareness of our emotions and skillful management of how we communicate them help us successfully steer through the roiling waters of intimacy.

Containment, mindful awareness, and skillful verbalization, though difficult to learn, can make life with others much easier and more satisfying. First step, as always, is to recognize unhelpful patterns such as ignoring difficult feelings or angry outbursts that allow us to discharge emotional tension at our partner's expense.

Consider these three scenarios:

1. Jim has a very demanding job and is also very sensitive and reactive emotionally. He believes in authenticity. If he has a bad day, he makes no attempt to hide this as he walks in the door. Often within seconds, he barks orders to the kids in the living room to turn off the TV and get to their homework. He then turns to his wife, Lucy, in the kitchen and asks her why she is letting them watch TV. Minutes after he's home, everyone in the family feels unhappy. Later, when he has calmed down a bit, Lucy comments that he seemed pretty upset when he came home. Jim

replies, "Well, you know how stressful my work is; today was just one of those days."

2. Susan grew up with a mother who raged often and loudly. She learned to turn down the volume of her experience in order to not feel emotional reverberations. She is very rational and prides herself on staying cool in any situation. She also has a very demanding job supervising a large team of people.

    Claire, her wife, can read her when she walks through the door. Often, Claire goes to greet Susan and encounters her stiffening body and a forced smile that signals "Don't touch me."

    Later, at dinner, when Claire asks Susan what happened at work, she'll say, "Nothing in particular."

    Claire will make one more try, something like "You seemed a little tense when you came home."

    And Claire will say, somewhat sharply, "No, not really."

3. Matt comes through the door, tense from a bad staff meeting at the end of the day. He walks hesitantly into the kitchen, aware that he's not in the mood to really greet his partner. Alex is happy Matt's home and eager to greet him but immediately sees the tension in his face.

    "Sorry," Matt says, "I'm not fit for human contact

right now. I think I'll go for a jog. Hopefully that will help."

"Okay," Alex responds. He's disappointed and angry that Matt's work, once again, has left him in not such a good mood. Alex briefly considers following him out of the kitchen to tell him so, then knows that will likely lead to an unpleasant and unproductive exchange. Instead, Alex returns to making dinner and decides to let it go.

In a few minutes Alex is back to neutral and having fun cooking. At dinner, and after a short jog and a shower, Matt is tired, but no longer angry. They chat pleasantly for a while about various social plans, then Alex asks, "Do you want to talk about work?"

"Not really, but I am getting weary of all the political jockeying that's going on there."

"Yeah, I know; me too. I'm getting tired of you being upset so much of the time."

"Me too," Matt responds, and they proceed to commiserate on that point for a few minutes before segueing into a talk about their daughter's new job.

Jim is an example of expressing negative emotions as they occur with the result that his kids and wife experience unpleasant emotional reactions. He has allowed his unhappiness to be contagious. He knows what he is feeling and acknowledges it, but in a way that causes further damage.

Susan is keeping her experience out of her awareness, which results in an inability to talk about it with her wife. Claire is emotionally sensitive and feels her partner's pain, but they cannot support and comfort each other due to Susan's unawareness.

Matt and Alex's handling of unpleasant emotions is an example of skillful containment followed by skillful communication. They each try, mostly successfully, to contain negative emotions while they work to understand and detoxify them. Having succeeded in regaining more neutral internal states, they then communicate to each other what they understand about these feelings and offer support.

Exercise: Emotional Contagion

In this exercise, you are going to use your mindfulness and containment skills to observe your own experience when in the presence of someone else's strong emotion. This might be your partner or someone else. Being with small children is a great way to practice!

1. The next time you are with someone who is having a very strong emotional response, pay close attention to your own experience. Remember that emotions may be experienced physically, mentally, or emotionally. And with contagion, you may experience the same emotion or something different in response.

2. *Reflect and write:*

• What do you think the other person was feeling?

- What did you feel in their presence?
- What was it like to contain and observe, rather than express?

3. Do not, in this case, talk about your experience; simply contain and observe.

CHAPTER 9

Too Little and Too Much

We vary as individuals in terms of both the types and intensity of our internal emotional responses, and, as well, in how we externally express our emotions. Some of this variability is nature (we were born that way), and some of it nurture (a result of the way that those around us handled emotions, their own and ours). Additionally, there are wide cultural differences in emotional expression. We are all familiar with the stereotypes of fiery Italians or taciturn Scandinavians.

There is also gender bias. Men are, unfortunately, still socialized not to express their emotions or emotional needs. I once sat with a couple when the wife said, with some sadness, "I just want to feel that you want to be with me." Her husband replied somewhat impatiently, "Of course I want to be with you. I'm still here, aren't I?" *Ouch!* He's very uncomfortable with the idea of overt talk about tender feelings; she feels she is in an emotional desert.

In this example, there is also a language barrier. They will both benefit if he can become comfortable with overt expression, and she can learn to turn up the amplifier on what he does offer. He may also be uncomfortable with her more dramatic emotional expressions. She needs to learn that he can hear her expressions of emotion better at lower intensities. And he needs to cultivate the ability to be less reactive when she goes over the mark.

TOO LITTLE

As you have been experimenting with aperture awareness and dialogue, you may have discovered that you have trouble knowing what you are experiencing. Connecting with your partner starts with learning to connect with yourself.

Sometimes people have a general absence of experience; they can't find their thoughts, their emotions, or their bodies during a conversation with their partner, and perhaps at other times also. They commonly notice that they feel nothing or numb when they go looking for how they feel. If, as children, our experience is too strong or we do not have enough support to tolerate it, we can learn to anesthetize ourselves, and some people learn this very well and very early.

For others, there is awareness but difficulty verbalizing. This can result in the impression, for you or for your partner, that you are lacking emotional experience. As noted, putting things into words helps us make sense of them and even to experience them. Without the ability to put emotions into words, you may feel you have a chaotic and unmanageable internal experience. Fortunately, it is possible to learn both the awareness and the verbalization.

Exercise: Interoceptive Awareness

For people with difficulty knowing their emotional experiences, focusing on physical sensations is a way to develop this awareness. I suggest that you do this exercise several times, until you start to get the hang of it. Then, in your next few dialogues, use these steps to tune in to what you sense in your body and express it to your partner in terms of the felt sensations. From there, it may be possible to translate into the more common terms of emotional experience.

1. Sit alone for a few minutes, five might be a good start, with nothing to do but tune in to what is going on inside your body.
2. What do you notice in the core of you, your chest and abdomen? What word or few words come to mind for the sensations you find there? Don't limit yourself to the typical emotion words; in fact, you are trying to use any descriptive word that comes to mind. Here are some prompts, but questions of your own may be even more helpful in your exploration:

    •   Hard or soft?
    •   Warm or cold?
    •   Dark or light?
    •   Still or moving?
    •   Pleasant or unpleasant?

3. As you keep your attention on this experience, how does it change?

    •   How is it affected by your breath?
    •   What else do you notice?

4. *Reflect and write.*

Teamwork for Feedback

Due to limbic resonance (see page 34, "Aperture and the Limbic System"), teamwork can be helpful in learning to sense and talk about your emotional experience. You may be able to use your partner's awareness to help you tune in to emotional experience that you are having trouble noticing. The teamwork of this practice can be challenging. You'll need to figure out what will work for you.

Consider this example and the possibilities for teamwork. Etta and Stan are having a talk about last night's dinner with another couple. In discussing one part of the evening, Etta comments that Stan got competitive with the other man. Soon after she mentions this, the conversation starts to get tense. Stan starts arguing with her. Etta gets angry, and soon they are raising their voices and grimacing at each other.

What's happening behind the scenes (and partly unconsciously) is that Etta is feeling anxious that Stan may have damaged the friendship with the other couple. Stan then gets anxious that Etta is displeased with him. Unaware of either his own or Etta's anxiety and vulnerability, Stan becomes angry and aggressive. Etta, also unaware of either of their vulnerabilities, then also becomes aggressive.

Here are two possible alternatives where they use teamwork:

1. When Etta notes that Stan got competitive with the other man, Stan catches himself on the way to arguing. He remembers that he and Etta had discussed the possibility (a hypothesis) that Etta gets critical of him when she is feeling vulnerable.

Stan then reminds Etta of this and asks her if she might be feeling something.

Etta sits with this for a minute and comes up with the possibility that she is feeling anxious and insecure. She really likes this other couple and is concerned about the friendship. Once Etta is aware of and able to state these feelings, Stan becomes less reactive to her comment. He then also acknowledges his own insecurity in response to her criticism.

2.   After Etta notes that Stan got competitive with the other man, Stan gets very quiet. Etta notices that she's getting tense. Then she remembers talking to Stan about how he gets quiet when he's upset. They had agreed to try to notice this and explore emotional reactions when it happens. She reminds Stan of this idea and asks him if she has said something that upset him.

Stan is able, after a few moments, to notice that the possibility of Etta being displeased with him has made him feel very insecure. Etta is then able to express concern for his feelings. She explains that her comment about Stan's behavior came from her feeling of insecurity in the relationship with the other couple.

In both these scenarios, Etta and Stan team up for mindfulness so that their emotional reactions become available for observation and verbalization. This kind of teamwork requires trust and also increases trust. The upward spiral in action.

Body Language

Another way to increase awareness of emotional experience is to make use of body language. Our body postures and gestures change when we're experiencing strong emotions. Many people fold their arms over their chest in a self-protective gesture. Others may gesticulate with their hands energetically. Others might break eye contact for extended periods. A subtle version of this is a barely noticeable, and unintentional, change in posture or facial expression. In poker, this is called a tell, and if read correctly, it signals other players of a person's reaction to their cards. The ability to conceal these reactions is what we mean by "poker-faced." In intimate relationships, this kind of concealment, whether conscious or unconscious, is a disadvantage and gets in the way of being understood by your partner.

Concealing emotions in this way may also inhibit self-knowledge. We learn what we are feeling as our body reacts, so inhibiting physical reactions, especially facial expressions, may decrease our awareness of emotion. Learning to be aware of your tell can be the doorway to knowing what you're feeling. And because these physical messages are so often unconscious, teamwork with your partner can be useful.

Exercise: Emotional Tells

This exercise involves teamwork and partner feedback. If you don't feel ready for the teamwork, you can start by doing the exercise on your own.

1. Spend a week or two paying close attention to the physical manifestations of your emotional reactions. Keep notes. Your partner should keep

their own notes about what they notice about your tells. During this period do not discuss your observations. This allows each of you to observe without being influenced.

2.   Schedule a time to discuss your observations. Record the results.

- What were your observations about your tells?
- What were your partner's observations?
- What were you surprised by?
- How do you feel about your partner being able to read your tells?

3.   Proceed with a week or two of noticing your tells during interactions with your partner. Try to describe what you are feeling in a word or two. You may notice a physical experience like tightness, or you may be able to find emotional words like *nervous* or *sad*.

You may want your partner to participate by giving you feedback when they notice a physical sign. If so, follow this process:
a) Your partner tells you what they notice and asks if you are feeling anything.
b) Take a minute or two to see if you can detect an emotion. You may easily know what it is, or you may not be able to find any internal correlation to their observation.
c) You then have a choice about whether to talk about what you notice. Both of you should respect this choice. It may or may not be the right time to try to communicate your feeling.

Follow the period of partner feedback with a week or two of asking them *not* to comment so you can see if you're now able to notice your own external behavior and use it to find your internal reaction.

4. *Reflect and write:*

    •   What behavior(s) were you tracking?
    •   Did your awareness of the external signal help you find your emotional experience?
    •   Did it seem to be linked to a particular emotion? Or was it a signal for a variety of emotions?

5. *Discuss.*

TOO MUCH

Some people have the opposite difficulty: intense internal or external responses that are too much for either you or your partner, or both. As with too little emotion, too much emotion is determined both by genetics and by your experiences.

Being part of a couple can be very stimulating, sometimes in a good way, but not always. People tend to couple with a person with whom they have a lot of resonance. The upside of this is that you easily feel connected. But, at times, your responses to your partner can be uncomfortably and unproductively strong.

The problems with too much emotional response are several. There is the discomfort itself. Then, in an effort to escape the discomfort, you may shut down—your aperture closes—resulting in difficulty processing. It becomes difficult to think, speak, or be aware of your environment, including your partner's responses and aperture.

Too much emotional experience can result in unbalanced communication. If one person is more adept at knowing what they feel and/or communicating those feelings, the other can start to feel there's no room for their emotional experience. Good dialogue needs various types of balance (see Chapter 5), and this is an important one. *Both* of you need to make sure there's room for the emotional responses of *each* of you.

Here are a few strategies to try.

Self-Soothing

We discussed earlier the distinction between holding your partner responsible for *their* actions and holding them responsible for *your* feelings and your recovery from difficult emotions. The expectation that your partner must soothe your uncomfortable feelings is often unrealistic. This *can* happen and can be lovely and loving. But when people are reliant on external soothing and assume that they cannot feel better until their partner does something, resentment develops for both people. The ability to make oneself feel better when uncomfortable is an important skill of internal self-management. Each of you needs to develop the ability to do this.

Related to the importance of self-soothing is the issue of urgency. Some people experience urgency for resolution when something has gone wrong. They feel that the only way to feel better is to engage and resolve things. This can lead to initiating or continuing difficult conversations when emotional discomfort is too high and apertures are closed. As you now know, that will likely make things worse.

We need to learn to feel better to talk, rather than talking to feel better.

By practicing not responding to the feeling of urgency, we discover that we can feel better even though the difficulty that caused pain is not resolved. Once we're feeling better, we're more able to engage in helpful conversation.

Using Your Mind

There are two cognitive strategies that have the power to help us calm our emotional storms. The first, *labeling*, has to do with finding a word or a few words for what we're feeling, as discussed in the "Verbalizing Emotion" section on page 171. Using fMRI, Matthew Lieberman found that when subjects assigned a one-word description to what they saw on angry or scared faces, they had less limbic activation, less emotional response.[1]

The second cognitive strategy is *reframing*. Our emotional reactions result from the story we tell ourselves, the meanings we assign to what is happening. Changing the story changes the emotions. In one study, Kevin N. Ochsner showed subjects a picture of people crying outside a church. Some subjects were told that the image was a wedding; others were told it was a funeral, and there were very different fMRI results. Those who thought they were seeing a wedding had more prefrontal cortex activation and a reduction in activation of the limbic system.[2]

In a downward spiral, partners' interpretations of each other's communications tend to be more like funerals and less like weddings. When you're upset by an interaction, considering the story you're telling yourself and the possibility that there are other interpretations is one way to calm the storm. (See the Skillful Handling of Misunderstandings exercise, page 123.) Additionally, the larger context will influence how you experience a difficult moment.

Finally, don't forget the power of distraction. Giving your mind something to work on other than the current injury or problem is a great way to interrupt limbic activity. Take a break and come back to the difficulties after the emotional storm has calmed.

> ### WHAT'S DETERMINING YOUR
> ### COGNITIVE FRAME?
>
> - Are you giving your partner the benefit of the doubt?
> - Are you influenced by the ways that this moment seems like moments in the past?
> - Are you considering your role in what is happening?
> - Are you influenced by either a desire to win or a desire to claim victimization?
> - Are you connected to your compassion, for yourself, and for your partner?

Using Your Body

Because your body is the source of signals that inform you about your feelings, you can change how you feel by making physical changes. Smiling, even if you don't feel it in the moment, actually makes people feel happier. Studies also show that posture influences how we feel in response to information. People receiving good news in a slumped posture felt less proud than those receiving the same news with an upright spine.[3] We also have abundant research showing the positive effects of being in nature and enjoying art.[4]

When you're feeling the difficulty of too much emotion, consider going for a walk, taking a swim or a bath, exercising, doing yoga, listening to music, painting a picture, or visiting a museum.

FLOODING

At a certain point of too much closing aperture and escalating emotional reaction, a cascade of neurophysiological responses is triggered.

THE PHYSIOLOGY OF FLOODING

- Secretion of neurotransmitters adrenaline and cortisol
- Increased heart rate and strength of heart contractions
- Constriction of arteries
- Lower blood oxygen
- Immunosuppression
- Increased amygdala activation (danger response)
- Decreased frontal lobe activation (planning and complex processing)
- Decreased ability to take in visual and auditory information[5]

This is the fight-flight-freeze response, also referred to as flooding, and it's very uncomfortable. You're drowning in emotions. Your body feels terrible; you can't think and you may feel your heart racing and pounding. You may notice sweating; clenching of the stomach, jaw, or other body parts; and feeling very cold or very warm. You may notice difficulty processing mentally. Emotionally, you're likely experiencing extreme fear, anger, or despair. Or there may be a sense of numbing or shutting down, emotionally, physically, and mentally.

Of this meltdown state, Dan Seigel says, "The middle prefrontal cortex—the region that calms the emotionally reactive lower limbic and brainstem layers—stops being able to regulate all the energy being stirred up, and the coordination and balance of the brain is disrupted. . . . We go down the 'low road,' moving directly from limbic impulse to speech and action, and detouring away from the prefrontal 'high road,' where we are flexible and receptive rather than inflexible and reactive."[6]

Once a person is flooded, it will take about twenty minutes from the start of active recovery for the chemical deluge to subside and to return to physiologic balance. In other words, twenty minutes of removing yourself from the upsetting situation and *not* thinking about how upset you are. Interestingly, men's recovery takes slightly longer than women's.[7] Flooding is very costly for individuals and for the relationship. In Gottman's research, frequent flooding is one of the predictors of divorce.[8]

Aperture awareness makes all the difference in learning to minimize flooding. People do not usually go instantly from wide-open apertures to flooding. Flooding happens when you ignore closing apertures. Continuing to talk with apertures of less than 5 generally results in apertures continuing to close, and because of limbic resonance, if one person's aperture is closing, the other's is usually not far behind. It then becomes more likely that one or both of you will end up flooded.

Worse yet is continuing to talk when one or both of you is flooded. This is almost certain to cause damage. Signs of flooding should elicit an immediate time-out of at least twenty minutes. Do not reengage in any way until both of you have returned to a state of emotional neutrality and aperture openness. Taking a time-out when you're flooded is particularly tricky as self-control, your response flexibility, goes to almost zero. (We will look at this more in the next chapter.) Thus, the importance of slowing down and pausing if apertures are closing.

If you find yourself in a relationship where either of you is unable or unwilling to learn to disengage before you harm each other, emotionally or physically, you should seek help. In no case should ongoing damaging behavior be accepted.

Exercise: What Does Flooding Feel Like?

What do you know so far about how you feel when you are flooded? For some of you this will be easy; you've experienced flooding and are very aware of what it's like. Others may not have experienced this, or you have not been able to stay aware enough to notice what you feel. Often, when people are flooded, observing is difficult. The goal of this exercise is to become more aware of what flooding feels like so you know when to take a time-out.

1. The following is a list of common subjective experiences of flooding. Record any that seem familiar to you.

    Emotional
    ___ I feel so angry that it is hard to control myself.
    ___ I feel so angry that I end up throwing or hitting something.
    ___ I feel so afraid that I can't stand it.
    ___ I feel so afraid that I have to leave the room quickly.
    ___ I feel like I have to hide.
    ___ I feel an intolerable amount of despair.
    ___ I feel as if everything is hopeless.

___I feel as if this relationship is hopeless.

___I feel numb.

___I try to calm down but cannot.

Mental

___I feel like my brain is jammed and I can't fig-
ure out what my partner just said.

___I feel as if my brain is jammed and I can't
think of what I want to say.

___I feel as if I can't make sense out of things.

___I am having thoughts of violence.

___I am having thoughts of running away.

___My brain seems to be thinking of things irrel-
evant to what is happening.

Physical

___My chest is tight.

___My stomach is knotted.

___My heart is racing.

___I am sweating.

___I feel cold and clammy.

___I am breathing very hard or very fast.

___I am holding my breath.

___Some parts of my body are tingling.

___I can't feel my body.

Behavioral

___I am talking louder than I want to.

___I am talking faster than I want to.

___I am interrupting more than is good.

___I try to speak, but the words that come out
don't make sense.

___I try to speak, but the words that come out
aren't what I meant to say.

___ I try to speak but can't.

___ I'm throwing things, slamming doors, hitting
things.

Write down anything else you can capture about
what it feels like when you are flooded.

2. Now, try to capture what you have noticed about
    the signs that your partner is flooded. These obvi-
    ously will be only physical and behavioral. Again,
    record as many as apply.

Physical

___ They cross their arms tightly over their chest.

___ They clench their hands.

___ They jiggle their legs.

___ Their face flushes.

___ Their face is pale.

___ They sweat.

___ They breathe very hard or very fast.

___ They hold their breath.

___ They make some repetitive body movement
(tapping a pencil very fast, etc.).

Behavioral

___ They talk louder than usual.

___ They talk faster than usual.

___ They interrupt more than is good.

___ They try to speak, but the words that come out
don't make sense.

___ They try to speak, but the words that come out
aren't what they meant to say.

___ They seem frozen, not responding.

___ They throw things, slam doors, hit things.

___I try to get my partner to calm down but cannot.

Make some notes about anything else you have observed in your partner when they are flooded.

3. Spend the next week paying close attention to possible flooding and record any additional observations about yourself or your partner during states of flooding.

Instant Flooding: The Sudden, Disproportionate Response

Many painful moments happen when one or both of you has a sudden, exaggerated negative response. You're suddenly flooded, with all the attendant difficulties of loss of cognitive skills, inability to communicate, physical distress, and feeling or acting out of control. As difficult as flooding is to deal with when it comes on gradually, it is even harder when it happens suddenly.

It might go something like this.

Nick: [Neutral tone, somewhat distracted.] What's for dinner?

Sharon: [Turning from the sink to glare at him and speaking with a tense voice.] What's for dinner?!

Nick: [Startled and wary.] Uh, yeah, what's for dinner?

Sharon: [Fully flooded, furious, eyes popping and yelling.] Are you kidding me?!

Nick: [Mentally scrambling to understand what he did wrong, feeling very afraid and thinking, *How did I ever end up with such a crazy nutjob for a wife?* He turns to beat a hasty retreat, muttering.] Just forget it.

So, what happened here? Sharon and Nick have been having increasing tension between them and very little time together since their twins were born ten months ago. Sharon's concern about the downturn of their relationship is amplified by the memory of her parents' painful divorce. She tried to get Nick to go to couples counseling, but he refused. Things got worse. Sharon started to feel angry at his seeming lack of interest in her and his refusal to go to therapy.

About a week ago, when Sharon tearfully complained of feeling unloved, Nick suggested they try having date nights. She felt a little better and looked forward hopefully to their first night out since the babies arrived. The evening of this difficult interaction was to have been the first date night.

In these situations, often the missing information that makes sense of what is happening is that your partner's reaction, though triggered by your behavior, is amplified by other factors, such as:

- Chronic difficulties in the relationship
- History of the specific trigger in the relationship
- History of painful events in other relationships with parents, siblings, or other partners
- Other current stresses
- Fatigue

Simple mistake: Nick forgot about date night. Amplifying circumstances: exhaustion, tension, decrease in relationship satisfaction, Nick's refusal to try couples therapy, Sharon's parents' divorce.

Mistakes in a relationship are normal and happen quite frequently, small ones often daily. Minus other difficulties, a response of some upset may be felt and expressed in proportion to the offense. But exaggerated responses will need special handling.

Learning to recognize them is the first step. The next step is accepting that special handling is required. The tendency when your partner has an exaggerated response is to become defensive and point out that what you did *should not* elicit this kind of response. Alternatively, you may go on the offensive, making it clear how ridiculous your partner is being. Perhaps you've discovered that neither of these is helpful.

The best response, as when dealing with actual explosives, is to back away and carefully consider your options. This is where mindfulness comes to your aid. Exercising your ability to contain and consider, you notice your reaction to your partner's sudden and unexpected flooding. You see the mismatch between your behavior and their response, likely meaning that the reaction is heightened by other factors.

If you move toward self-soothing rather than fight-flight-freeze, you can practice damage control. Perhaps you call for a time-out with reassurance that you will return to this at another time. Handling a crisis of sudden flooding well can strengthen your relationship.

CHAPTER 10

Impulses and Expression

Antonio Damasio, neuroscientist, says, "We are about as effective at stopping an emotion as we are at preventing a sneeze."[1] We do not become a better partner by preventing or controlling our emotions but by learning mindful awareness of them before they derail a conversation.

We've been talking about pausing for closing apertures and waiting for reopening to speak. But what about those times you "run the stop sign" of closing apertures? You may have found yourself unable to stop, even though you knew you were about to say something harmful. This is the difficulty we sometimes refer to as lack of impulse control, and it is possible to get better at pausing and mindfully choosing your next move to both limit damage and build trust. I'm going to describe two methods for learning these skills.

MINDFUL EXPRESSION METHOD A: EARLY WARNING SYSTEM

You have been practicing aperture awareness and using a 1–10 scale to describe different levels of openness. To develop an early warning system, I want to discuss aperture in terms of four different zones: green, yellow, orange, and red.

For the purposes of this method, the green zone, roughly 6–10, means you're good to go. You're feeling fairly calm, relaxed, and interested in contact. You are capable of generosity, empathy, listening, and learning. In the green zone, it is unlikely that you will be out of control with harmful impulse expression.

In the yellow zone, 4–5, you're starting to close down, but with a little skill and collaboration, you can exercise enough control to avoid damaging behaviors and pull yourself back into the green zone.

In the orange zone, 2–3, it is becoming increasingly likely that your expressions will be less than mindful and less than skillful, and may be harmful. You may be able to effectively reopen, but, as your aperture falls below 4, reopening becomes more difficult. You're on the way to red.

The red zone, 1, is flooding. Being in control when you are flooded is as impossible as not being swept away in a tsunami. To avoid harmful interactions in flooding you must discontinue contact, and this is extremely hard to do when you are flooded.

With the early warning system you learn to slow down or stop before losing the ability to do so. The key to staying out of the red is to stay out of the orange, and the key to staying out of the orange is skillful handling of the yellow zone.

For some people, entering the yellow zone is like stepping on the banana peel: suddenly you have crashed, and you didn't even see it coming. If this is true for you, then in the early stages of gaining control, only the green zone will be safe, and any dip into yellow means you need to discontinue contact. As you strengthen your ability to stay aware and mindful, it may become possible to dip into yellow or even orange, ride out the waves of emotion, and return to green without harming or needing a time-out. The key to success is willingness to be a learner and to respect your limits.

Exercise: Moving from Yellow to Green

The foundational skill here is learning to keep track of your own aperture. You need to know when you are in each zone. If you feel that you are not yet able to maintain awareness of your aperture, return to the exercises of Chapter 1. If you suspect your difficulty may be due to limited awareness of your emotions, "Too Little" (page 181) in Chapter 9 and the exercises there may be helpful. When you feel that you are able to have some awareness of your emotions and aperture, you are ready for this next practice of awareness of early warning signs.

Some topics are so difficult that we feel ourselves moving from green to yellow or beyond just thinking about them. Save these for later. Note that you may also have opportunities to practice these skills when not actually in dialogue with your partner. You may get triggered by something that happens at work or while driving. Be alert for chances to practice.

1. For this exercise, you will need a topic that is somewhat, but not too, challenging, and about forty minutes.
2. Make sure you're each in the green zone to begin.
3. As soon as you feel your aperture shift to the yellow zone, 4–5 instead of 6 or above, ask for a time-out to study what is happening.

It is not always easy to press Pause in the middle of an important conversation. You will need to work together to do this experiment and explore the benefits. It may help to remember that once flooding happens, it will take a full twenty minutes or more before you can continue without harmful effects. Small pauses to recover open apertures are the key to being able to continue.

This is similar to what you did in the exercise Aperture Recovery (page 70). But instead of teamwork with your partner to get back to green, you are going to work with yourself. Tell your partner you'll let them know when you're ready to continue. Then consider the following:

- What are you feeling?
- How strong is it?
- When did you start feeling it?
- Was there a particular trigger?

When one of you asks for a time-out, it's a good time for the other to, likewise, check their aperture.

4. Next, see if you can move back to green. This is like the process of dealing with flooding, but at lower states of distress. Do whatever helps you feel better. This is self-soothing practice and a chance to experiment.

It's also, of course, a chance for increasing mindfulness. When you pause to reopen aperture, you have a chance to notice any resistance that arises to doing this. Perhaps it feels unnatural, or too vulnerable?

5. When you are back in the green zone, consider whether there is anything you or your partner might do differently with this conversation that would make it less distressing to you. Then let your partner know you are ready to try again, discussing changes the two of you might make to how you are talking.

6. Repeat as needed. You may need to repeat this process many times; this learning is iterative, challenging, and time-consuming. At some point it will become easier to recognize the shift from green to yellow, take action, and get back to green before continuing.

7. *Reflect and write:*

•   What was challenging about this exercise?
•   Did you notice any feelings or thoughts that arose, such as fear of being hurt, or concerns about being controlled by your partner or about losing authenticity? Other concerns?
•   What seemed to work best for you in terms of self-soothing?
•   If your partner called for such a time-out, what were your reactions? How did you use the time?
•   Anything else you learned?

8. *Discuss.*

Moving from Orange to Green

To conduct hard conversations without avoiding conflict, you need to be able to tolerate the discomfort of being in the yellow zone without slipping into orange. This means that, while partially closed, you are able to slow down, stay mindfully aware, and respond in ways that do not make things worse for you or your partner. But you may, at times, slip into the orange zone. Now you are going to practice recovering from that.

Exercise: Moving from Orange to Green

You're going to experiment with observing and handling the moment when yellow (aperture of 4–5) turns to orange (aperture of 2–3). Choose a topic that involves the right amount of difficulty for you to be able to practice moving into yellow and then, possibly, orange. (Slips into red may happen as you practice. Be prepared to execute on the plan for flooding—full time-out of at least twenty minutes.)

1. Allow forty minutes for this conversation.
2. Make sure that you are each in the green zone to begin your dialogue. As you talk, experiment with allowing yourself to move from yellow to orange before you call a time-out. Then call for your time-out, and tell your partner you'll let them know when you're ready to continue. For a slip into the orange zone, you will probably need more time to observe and also to reopen. (As before, it's a good time for the other person to, likewise, check their aperture.)
3. Now consider:

    *   What are you feeling?
    *   How strong is it?
    *   When did you start feeling it?

- Were you aware of the move from green to yellow? Was there a particular trigger?
- What caused you to move from yellow to orange? Did something further trigger this?

4. Now see if you can move back to green. Do whatever helps you feel better and more open. In the beginning, a slip into orange may mean that you need twenty minutes or more to get all the way back to green. When you are back in the green zone, consider whether there is anything you or your partner might do differently with this conversation that would make it less distressing to you. Then let your partner know you are ready to try again, discussing the potential changes.

5. Repeat as needed. As before, this learning process may require many repetitions.

6. *Reflect and write:*

- What was challenging about this exercise?
- How was this different from pausing for yellow?
- What did you notice about your feelings and thoughts?
- What seemed to work best for you in terms of self-soothing?
- How long did it take to move back from orange to green?
- If your partner called for a time-out, what were your reactions? How did you use the time?
- Anything else you learned?

7. *Discuss.*

MINDFUL EXPRESSION METHOD B:
VERBALIZATION AND ACCOUNTABILITY

Method A strengthens aperture awareness, using it to stop the action before you become overwhelmed and out of control. Method B is for those out-of-awareness, out-of-control expressions that can happen at any time, not just during dialogue.

Verbalization and accountability are helpful for those times when you have identified a behavior that injures your partner but you are unable to inhibit it. Giving voice to what's going on cultivates mindfulness of the impulse before expression, thus allowing you to gain conscious control of unwanted behaviors.

Neuroscience tells us that speaking activates more neural circuits than thinking, making it easier to focus and process information. "When you develop language that describes an activity . . . it is more likely that you can catch yourself about to do something before taking action."[2]

Accountability is the harnessing of intentionality to direct our future actions. Note that this is different from willpower. When we try to change our behavior, we often misstep in thinking that sheer willpower is what is needed. But we know from the research of Roy Baumeister and others that the ability to will ourselves to do things is extremely limited. "The list of situations and tasks that are now known to deplete willpower is long and varied."[3] When we try to control our behavior with willpower, we often fail. When we understand how to use intentionality, we have much more ability to affect future behavior.

Example: Karla has a habit of criticizing Dave in front of other people when she's angry with him. Dave, understandably, is hurt by this. At first when he tries to talk to her about it, she gets defensive and says that he is being overly sensitive, that she hardly ever does this. In other words, she is pretty *unaware* of it. After a few difficult talks, she comes to think that maybe he's right. She also agrees that if this is happening, it's not good.

This example contains all three aspects of the repair process (page 153). Karla establishes empathetic connection around the behavior that is injuring Dave (Aspect 1); they discuss each of their experiences and find they don't agree about what is happening (Aspect 2); and she agrees with him about what the desired behavior is (Aspect 3). She can't agree to change her behavior yet because she's not aware of it. What she can do is agree to a period of investigation ("Offering to Investigate," page 136; Investigating Hypotheses exercise, page 137).

Now, she invites Dave to *gently* point out the behavior. After a few of these assists, Karla sees what she's doing and decides to change. (In Part Four we will discuss aspects of this teamwork in more detail.)

Karla is able to see her behavior *if* Dave points it out. Now, Karla must become aware of the behavior *without assistance*. In the beginning there will probably be a lag time—hours, even days—between the behavior and her recognition of it. It might go something like this:

On Tuesday morning, Karla is thinking about last night's dinner with friends and suddenly realizes that when they discussed buying a new car, she was pretty opinionated and made fun of Dave's interest in a van. As soon as she realizes this, she texts Dave, "I just realized that the way I handled your comments about the van was an example of what you were talking about. Very sorry. I'm working on it." The lag time here between her behavior and her awareness is about twelve hours. An interesting thing now begins to happen: the act of acknowledging, taking responsibility, and verbalizing starts to shorten this interval.

That night at a ball game with his parents, she makes a

snide remark about Dave not scheduling plans in advance. A few minutes later she suddenly realizes what she said. She then leans toward him, kisses him on the cheek, and whispers, "Sorry," in his ear. Now the lag time is a few minutes.

Soon she will be catching herself *before* she makes the hurtful, critical comment. This is the moment of mindfulness, during which she is able to observe her impulse, pause, and make a conscious decision about what she wants to do. Having decided that she doesn't want to say hurtful things to Dave, she might decide instead to take a break for a few minutes (containment), make a note about a possible future dialogue, and return to enjoying his company.

Starting wherever you are in your awareness of the behavior you want to change, the process of consistently holding yourself accountable and putting words to your awareness results in becoming aware before you act. So, at first you might become aware a few hours later, then a few minutes later, then a few seconds later, until finally you're aware just *before* the behavior, and voilà! You now have mindfulness and can make a choice to handle the emotional impulse in some other way.

Exercise: Method B: Verbalization and Accountability

This is not a timed experiment; it's a process, as shown in the example with Karla.

1. To begin, identify a target behavior, something your partner finds hurtful, that you agree should not be happening, and you're either unaware of it or feel unable to gain control.
2. Enlist the help of your partner to point it out, agreeing, as Karla did, to be open to a period of

observation and learning. Your partner notes the behavior, without any additional comments or criticism. It's important that this is simply a moment of assisted awareness, not a time to discuss. (See also "The Arc of Change" on page 246.)

3. After the period of assisted observation, ask your partner to stop pointing out the behavior. You need a chance to notice it yourself, which initially will involve some delay between the behavior and becoming aware.

4. An important aspect of this method is that you hold yourself accountable *every time* you notice the behavior and that you acknowledge and apologize *as soon as* you have noticed. With this mindful awareness, you can now practice containment of the feelings, choosing not to do the behavior.

5. Once you've succeeded, you may still occasionally slip. In which case, you once again quickly acknowledge and apologize.

Keep track of your learning with the following notes:

• Target behavior _____
• Date you agree to investigate the behavior _____
• Date you agree to change the behavior _____
• Date you ask your partner to discontinue assists in awareness _____
• Date you first noticed on your own _____
• Behavior-awareness interval the first time you noticed the behavior on your own _____
• Behavior-awareness interval the second time you noticed on your own _____
• Behavior-awareness interval the third time you

noticed on your own _____
- Behavior-awareness interval the fourth time you noticed on your own _____
- Length of time between *first* independent awareness of behavior and first time you caught yourself *before* behavioral expression _____

6. *Reflect and write:*

- What was difficult?
- What was fun?
- What was surprising?
- Other things you learned?

7. *Discuss.*

CHAPTER 11

Anger

Anger is not just another emotion. Anger can be a powerful, potentially destructive force and a major problem in some relationships. Like fear, anger is part of our instinctive, defensive fight-flight-freeze response to feeling threatened. We often feel anger in response to other emotions and often do not even notice the emotions that triggered the anger response. Anger can be very toxic, and the experience and expressions of it need to be carefully, mindfully handled. Containment of anger can be particularly difficult as the experience is so uncomfortable. We want to get rid of it by expressing it immediately. Which of course only extends or transfers it to our partner.

This chapter offers tools and exercises so that you can understand and recognize your anger, take responsibility for it, and transform it into something that allows for reconnection with your partner.

One of my favorite understandings of anger is that of Thich Nhat Hanh, a Vietnamese Buddhist monk and skillful teacher.

Thich Nhat Hanh advised that we acknowledge our anger and the suffering it causes us. Rather than suppress it, he tells us to take good care of it. He suggests that we be very aware of our experience of anger and that, when we have become peaceful enough, we go to our partner and tell them, "Darling, I am angry, I suffer."[1] The part about "when we have become peaceful enough" is important—but so challenging that it almost sounds ironic, though he does not mean it that way.

Anger expressed *un*peacefully can injure. In aperture terms, he is suggesting that we practice aperture awareness, containment, mindful awareness of our experience, and expression only once our aperture has reopened. There is a great deal of difference between communicating *while* we are angry and communicating *about* our anger after the hot wave of it has passed.

Thich Nhat Hanh suggests that we let our beloved know we are angry with them within twenty-four hours, reminiscent of the biblical edict from Ephesians 4:26: "Let not the sun set on your anger." He suggests that if we cannot arrive at enough peace to express it calmly within twenty-four hours, we write it down. When ready, he advises that we say three things to our beloved:

1. *Darling, I am angry, I suffer.*
2. *I am doing my best.*
3. *Please help me.*

As you read these statements and imagine saying them or hearing them, I suspect that several things become clear: that this handling of anger will be consistent with loving your partner, that this approach will not further the harm, and that arriving at enough peacefulness to express anger this way will go a long way to dissolving your anger.

Notice that an underlying assumption is that, though your

partner may have triggered anger, your anger is not their fault or their responsibility. Sometimes this can be particularly difficult when you're angry; you can feel like "You broke it, you fix it." Like most defensive responses this can feel satisfying in the moment, yet it is not particularly helpful.

Anger is suffering and we deserve compassion, from ourselves and our partner. This is very different from the all-too-common assumption, often less than conscious, that for anger we deserve the perks of being a victim, including that the other person is to blame and should be punished.

When anger does get triggered, containment is important—an example of the idea that you need to feel better to talk instead of talking to feel better. This means that you let yourself fully feel the anger, feel compassion for your suffering, and try to discover the emotions that triggered the anger. It's not your partner's behavior that triggered the defensive response of anger, but your *emotional reaction* to their behavior. You may later want to discuss their behavior and changes you would like, but holding your partner responsible for your uncomfortable state of anger makes this harder and delays your understanding and self-compassion.

Another common pattern is that some people can only assert themselves in the heat of anger. This has the predictable result of triggering a fight-flight-freeze response from the partner. Both apertures close, and either a hurtful conversation ensues or both people run away quickly. This reinforces the belief that it is unsafe and unwise to bring up difficult things. If either of you has this pattern, it will be important to learn how to talk about differences and conflict at times when you're *not* angry. Learning to do this will, over time, decrease the frequency and intensity of anger, as well as the mishandling of it. And your partner will have a much better chance of understanding your message delivered with less anger.

As you open yourself to self-compassion for this miserable

experience you are having, without holding your partner responsible, at some point your aperture reopens and something resembling Thich Nhat Hanh's approach is possible. You can tell your partner about your anger and other feelings in a way that's more likely to help them be open, compassionate, and willing to discuss what happened.

For example: Jim and Linda are talking about summer vacation. Linda brings up her concerns that they may not have a good time in Hawaii since they didn't have a good time there last year. Jim instantly gets angry. How dare she remind him that it was his fault that the vacation did not go well! If he expresses this aggressively and immediately, Linda will very likely get angry back, or she may declare that he is impossible to talk to and end the conversation.

But what happens if Jim, instead of expressing the anger, contains his emotion and tries to understand his reaction? He may discover that her comment triggered shame and sadness since he feels that last year he was depressed and irritable, which made everyone miserable. He is angry at Linda for triggering these painful emotions. As he sits with this, his anger becomes less intense and he feels more sadness and regret.

Imagine what might ensue if he were then able to say to Linda, "Darling, I am angry, I suffer. I am doing my best. Please help me." Linda might respond compassionately, "Gee, I'm really sorry. What was it that made you angry?" He then explains. She may then be able to express caring for his difficulty and suggest that maybe they need to talk more about the last vacation before trying to plan the next one.

The process here is to:

- Contain the anger
- Try to understand the vulnerable emotions that triggered it

- Delay expression until the anger subsides and
  your aperture is open

Anger is one of the most difficult things to learn to handle in a nondestructive way. It may take you a while. Be patient with yourself and with your partner.

For the exercises with anger, we will break it down into three types: small anger, large anger, and chronic or long-standing anger.

SMALL ANGER

Small anger means a mild to moderate anger gets triggered, your aperture closes (but not all the way), and you are not flooded. Sometimes we use words like "frustrated" or "irritated" to distinguish small angers from larger angers. As always, the distinction between a reaction uncomfortable enough to close your aperture partially and one that sends you into the red zone of being flooded is important. Dealing with these smaller angry reactions uses the skills you have been learning: containment, mindfulness, aperture awareness, self-compassion, and waiting for your aperture to reopen before trying to communicate your feelings.

Exercise: Small Anger Containment

It is perhaps unwise that you and your partner intentionally trigger anger in each other in order to practice. So, you will need to review the instructions here and be ready to try this the next time the opportunity arises.

1. The next time you find yourself triggered to small amounts of anger, ask for a pause in the conversation.

2. Do not allow your partner to help or interrupt you. Simply sit there feeling your anger. Open yourself to self-compassion for this miserable experience you are having without holding your partner responsible for it.

3. Then try to discover the emotions that triggered the anger. Ask yourself, "What else am I feeling?"

4. When your aperture reopens to at least a 5, tell your partner about your anger and other feelings.

5. *Reflect and write:*

- If you had spoken immediately after you got angry, what might you have said to your partner?
- What was it like to contain your anger, delaying expression? What did you notice in your body? In your thoughts?
- Were you able to understand what emotions triggered the anger?
- What were they?
- Were you able to understand what triggered the other emotions?
- What was your experience as you practiced self-compassion?
- How long did it take you to get back to an aperture of 5 or better?
- How did you talk about your experience after your aperture reopened?

6. *Discuss.*

LARGE ANGER

Large anger means your aperture completely closes and you are flooded—the red zone. As discussed on page 191, flooding almost always involves anger, fear, or numbness as our amygdala takes over and we go into fight-flight-freeze. So, by large anger, I mean an anger that's this intense. Also, be aware that small events or issues can trigger large anger—it is not about the magnitude of the *trigger*, but the magnitude of the *anger*. Some people make it harder for themselves to deal with large anger by thinking that they shouldn't be so angry, that they are overreacting. Remember that you cannot control your emotional responses. Thinking you can gets in the way of mindful awareness and response flexibility.

Exercise: Large Anger Containment

As it is especially unwise to intentionally trigger large anger in each other, this is another exercise that you should review and be ready to use at the next opportunity.

1. When you notice that you are in the grips of this larger anger, tell your partner that you're flooded and will need to discontinue the conversation for at least twenty minutes.
2. Go somewhere you can be alone. Taking a walk is helpful. Let yourself fully feel your anger. This does not mean fanning the flames by perseverating on what your partner did. It means being aware of the anger as you experience it. Then try to open yourself to self-compassion for this miserable experience, this suffering, you are having without holding your partner responsible for it.

3. You may not be able to access the other emotions that triggered the anger until the intensity begins to subside and your aperture recovers a bit. As this happens, ask yourself, *What else am I feeling?* Continue until your aperture reopens, to at least a 5.

4. Approach your partner to request a talk about what happened for you. In this talk you should focus on describing your experience, rather than describing your partner's behavior. In this talk you may get angry again. In that case, repeat this or the exercise for small anger.

5. *Reflect and write:*

• What was it like to contain your anger, delaying expression? What did you notice in your body? In your thoughts?

• How long did it take for you to recover enough to be aware of other emotions that triggered the anger? What were they?

• Were you able to understand what behaviors of your partner triggered the other emotions? What were they?

• What was your experience as you practiced self-compassion?

• How long did it take you to get back to an aperture of 5 or better?

• When you tried to discuss your experience with your partner, did you get angry again?

• How was it different from the first time?

6. *Discuss.*

CHRONIC OR LONG-STANDING ANGER

Sometimes it can be especially hard to let go of anger. There are various reasons for this. Anger can make us feel powerful, righteous, in control, safe from future harm, or as though we're rectifying things by punishing. Anger makes us feel safe from other more vulnerable feelings of loss, sadness, uncertainty, or abandonment. It's helpful to consider these extra reasons you might be reluctant to feel less angry.

Anger is often a protest against something we find unacceptable. We feel unable to change something important, and feeling angry about it allows us not to feel impotent. We maintain a sense of wholeness as an individual by protesting. Sometimes, ongoing anger allows people to stay in relationships that are painful to them but which they feel unable to change or leave. This might be the situation for children with their parents or it might be true of some adult relationships. Anger can be a way of holding on. We even see this in people's angry reactions to losing someone through death. In order to completely grieve, we need to be able to stop hanging on with anger.

I have often worked with couples for whom staying angry was a way of protecting themselves from the fear of the relationship dissolving. Sometimes the answer to "Why is it hard for you to let go of your anger?" is "Because I'm afraid that I might leave." And sometimes, when couples stop being angry, they do find that the relationship is really over. But often, they let go of the anger and find the more vulnerable feelings that allow them to reconnect, heal, and build a better and stronger relationship.

Being willing to face this fear of loss to find out what is possible takes a lot of courage.

Exercise: Anger as Protection

This exercise may help you free yourself from long-standing anger. If, as you face the anger, you find fear, especially fear of losing the relationship, you may want to consider consulting a therapist, either individually or as a couple. Staying angry as a way of dealing with fear is very painful, soul depleting, and ultimately unsuccessful.

1. In advance of a conversation with your partner, consider these questions:

   - What is the anger you feel that's been hard to get free of?
   - What's the vulnerability that this anger might be protecting you from?

2. Discuss this vulnerability with your partner. As you do, pay close attention to what you're feeling, and especially to moments when vulnerability is replaced by anger. When you feel this, use the instructions from the previous exercises to contain and understand the anger and the other feelings.
3. *Reflect and write.*
4. *Discuss.*

CONSIDER CO-CREATION

In cases where someone feels stuck with long-standing anger that simply will not budge, there's a bit of magic in returning to the idea that everything in the relationship is a co-creation, the process of working together to create. Even though you may not see any part you have played in creating the situation that made you angry, return to the basic assumption that the two of you are linked in a system.

This often lessens the intensity of the anger and allows reopening. It's as if ongoing anger is being maintained by dividing your couple into the "right" or "good" person (you, the angry person) and the "wrong" or "bad" person (your partner). Soften this polarity and the anger may melt to a more manageable size. Notice that I don't say this removes the anger. You still have work to do. But remembering to entertain the possibility of co-creation often changes anger from a solid wall of rage to something that you can work with together. (More on this in Part Four.)

Consider the following questions:

- What is the long-standing anger that you are suffering from?
- What do you suspect about your partner's role in creating the situation that led to this anger?
- Do you have any ideas about your role in creating the situation that led to this anger?
- If not, can you entertain the possibility that somehow you have participated in creating the circumstances that have led to your anger?
- What is it like to be open to this possibility?

Exercise: A Dialogue About Co-Creation

A conversation about your distress as something the two of you have produced together is different from talking to your partner as if they *caused* your experience. To solve the puzzle of co-creation, you must each work to hear, undefensively, what your partner has to say about your part of the problem.

1. Invite your partner to a dialogue where the two of you try to understand the interactive pattern that is producing your upset. Start with the intention to collaborate to discover together. Be aware that it's likely you each will have a better view of the other's contribution than of your own.
2. Take a half hour to an hour to try to figure it out, using the tools you know for keeping apertures open.
3. *Reflect and write.*
4. *Discuss.*

PART FOUR

Learning and Change

Treat people as if they are what they ought to be and you help them to become what they are capable of being.

—Attributed to Johann Wolfgang von Goethe[1]

CHAPTER 12

How People Change

Couples often ask me, "Can people really change?" On the one hand, they're in my office because they believe, or at least want to believe, that they can change. On the other hand, they are very dubious about this possibility—afraid of change, afraid that they cannot change, afraid of the risk and vulnerability of trying to change.

Couples are pessimistic about change when they've been trying, sometimes for a long time, and have not succeeded. They often arrive at my door very discouraged. As with anything in life, succeeding depends on trying with the right methods. No matter how many times you try to shoe a horse with an egg, you will never succeed. Furthermore, concluding that the lack of success means there is something wrong with either the egg or the horse would be a serious misinterpretation of the results.

A better question is: Under what conditions do people change? This chapter is an exploration of some of the conditions for change. Understanding the change process, combined with the right skills, can greatly improve your success at creating changes you want.

WE ARE VERY GOOD AT CHANGE— ALSO NOT SO GOOD AT CHANGE

Couples' skepticism about change is interesting, since these same people do believe in *learning*, which, if you think about it, is another word for the kinds of changes couples are wondering about. Often what we mean when we say that people don't change is that we do not expect people to grow and learn past a certain age. The belief that growth, learning, and change happen only in children influences couples' expectations of what is possible.

Until recently we thought that the creation of neurons and their connections was an intensive process in the first few years of life, with some major revisions in adolescence. Thereafter, changes were thought to consist mainly of losses. But this expectation is both wrong and a recipe for unhappiness. In fact, the brain's capacity for learning and change— neuroplasticity—has been found to be vast and to continue throughout adulthood.

We now understand that while neuroplasticity slows down, it never stops. Throughout our lives our brains maintain the capabilities of neuroplasticity, including making new neurons, forming new connections, deleting connections, and reassigning whole brain areas to new functions. And because these changes happen in response to our experiences, we can participate actively in this process by choosing and shaping our experiences.

There are also aspects of our neurology that can make

change difficult. These are not absolute impediments, but we need to know about them and learn how to work with them.

Our survival has always depended on being able to decrease the uncertainties of life. Wired into our systems is a discomfort with uncertainty and a tendency to predict the future from the past. Predictions based on the past provide a way to navigate efficiently and safely through aspects of our environment that are, often, predictably the same, including our fellow humans' behaviors.

In the face of uncertainty our expectations are also influenced by the neurochemistry of expectations. Have you ever felt that there is risk involved in expecting good things and that your pessimism may be a way of hedging your bets? Well, you're right; expectations involve certain calculated risks. Let's look at how the odds are stacked in your brain.

- In general, positive expectations generate dopamine, the neurochemical of happiness.
- Met expectations yield a mild dopamine reward.
- Exceeded expectations yield a strong dopamine reward.
- Unmet expectations create a big dopamine drop and a strong threat response.[1]

In looking at the neurological biases for keeping your positive expectations in check, it is clear why we can feel at risk in expecting positive change. When things are going badly in a relationship, predictions about what will happen next (based on what has happened in the past and on hedging our bets) will be negative. These predictions become self-fulfilling prophesies; we tend to behave in ways that make our predictions come true. In this way we make positive changes less likely. If you want to see if things can change for the better, you must stop making and believing your own fearful predictions that things will go poorly.

Doing the Right Experiment

Openness to change and renewed hope feel extremely risky when your relationship is in a downward spiral. Everything is signaling that the ship is going down and you had best find a lifeboat and start rowing away before you get sucked under. You don't want to be disappointed, you don't want to be a fool, and you don't want to get hurt. As you consider whether to make a run for it or renew your efforts, you are looking for reassurance that the risks of trying again will pay off. In a downward spiral, you look at your partner's behavior and your interactions and feel anything but reassured.

It's important to understand that what you are seeing is the product of the downward spiral. We are all capable of a range of behaviors. We do best under conditions of trust, positive expectations, respect, and feeling valued. Clearly not the conditions present in the downward spiral. What you are seeing is your partner at their worst, under stressful conditions involving lack of trust, love, and support. While this is good to know, it does not tell you what they are capable of at their best. So, if you have decided to leave and are building your case, tallying up all your partner's flaws will help you do that. But do not mistake this for an understanding of what they, and you, might be capable of if you reverse the spiral.

The only way to find out if something better is possible is to do the right experiment. This means taking the risk of suspending your negative predictions and raising your expectations. Then be prepared, with mindfulness, to notice all the moments when your thoughts, feelings, or actions are being influenced by negative predictions creeping in.

Does this expose you to the risk of disappointment? Yes, of

course. That's why we call it a risk! If you're working to change the relationship for the better, you are, ipso facto, investing in the possibility of change. You do not know yet if your investment will pay off. What you can know is that *not* taking this risk has a predictable outcome of failing to move forward to learn and change together.

THE VISION

Each of us holds a heartfelt longing for an ideal relationship with a life partner. Sometimes we know what it is; occasionally we've even talked openly about it. Often it lives inside us, only partially guessed at.

We are most aware of this vision when we fall in love or decide to get married. But you don't get the relationship you want by choosing the right partner, scheduling a caterer, or putting a ring on your beloved's finger.

I often hear the story of couples deciding their dreams for their relationship are naive and unrealistic. They've encountered the difficulties of being in a committed relationship and a noticeable gap between what they're experiencing and what they had hoped for. They've decided that real relationships aren't capable of fulfilling their dreams. They look around at others' relationships and see confirmation of this. (How many people do you know who have the relationship you want to have?) They give up on their dreams and try to be realistic.

The secret to a great relationship is understanding that the vision is what you are *learning to do.* To realize your dreams, your commitment to each other must include a commitment to learning. Your vision gives you the motivation and courage. Without an inspiring vision, the work of relationship is too hard to sustain without exhaustion and resentment. You simply can't do it by aiming for something merely acceptable,

something far less than what you really want. In order to do all
the hard work and the hanging in there that a committed, intimate relationship requires, you need more than perspiration;
you need inspiration.

Exercise: The Vision

1. Each of you writes a description of your vision for
    this relationship. This is not a description of what
    you think is realistic, possible, normal, or enough.
    This is a description of everything you wish for. It
    is also not a description of your ideal *partner.* We
    often think that our partner is the supplier of all
    the wonderful things we want. This is quite differ-
    ent from imagining what you wish the two of you
    could create together.

2. Put your vision description aside for a day or
    two, then each of you interviews your partner
    for about fifteen minutes. Ask them to describe
    their ideal relationship. If you feel that they're
    not allowing themselves to say everything they
    really want, encourage them toward this kind of
    description.

3. *Reflect and write:*

    •   What was difficult for you about this exercise?
    •   What feelings did it generate?
    •   What was it like to share it with your partner?
    •   What was it like to hear your partner's vision?
    •   How did you feel?

4. *Discuss.*

THE POWER OF *YET*

Notice the difference in your responses to the following two sentences:

- We can't stop fighting.
- We can't stop fighting *yet*.

What do you notice about your aperture in response to each?

Or these:

- I can't get over the hurt they caused.
- I can't get over the hurt they caused *yet*.

Or:

- They don't understand me.
- They don't understand me *yet*.

In each pair, one statement will inhibit change; the other will support it. The first is a description of past experience with an implication that the past will continue and become your future, the self-fulfilling prophesy. The second, with the addition of "yet," is a description of past experience plus an expectation that things may be different in the future. Successful participation in change requires both a realistic understanding of what has been true and a willingness to suspend disbelief that, even after a frustrating time of repeating undesirable behaviors, change is possible.

Exercise: The Power of Yet

One of the right conditions for change is the belief that change is possible. When we speak about what is true for us, we're expressing and also listening and influencing our future. When we describe our frustrations with our partners or ourselves and add "yet," we remind ourselves that change is a process and that we have the ability to change.

1. Make a list of the skills you feel you do not yet have that would be helpful in your relationship.
2. At the end of each description add the word "yet." Example: I am not patient enough yet.
3. Read your lists out loud to each other, slowly, paying attention to how you feel as you hear your current limits expressed in this form.
4. *Reflect and write.*
5. *Discuss.*

CHANGE AND ACCEPTANCE

Though we often think of acceptance as what we do *instead* of change, it is actually a vital part of successful change. A friend once said to me about her marriage: "I've tried so hard to just accept him and not try to change him." To her surprise, my response was "Why?!"

She was surprised because much of the wisdom of relationships has focused on acceptance. Often couples are told that their unhappiness comes from a lack of acceptance of each other as they are. We have worked hard to understand the importance of not expecting our mate to be perfect, meet all our needs, fill all our emptiness. This is indeed wisdom, but it is incomplete.

Acceptance of people as they are includes understanding that healthy adults learn and change. In relationships, we need to be able to distinguish between acceptance as a precondition for change and acceptance that embraces stasis—which is really resignation. Acceptance and change are not opposites but actually two aspects of learning and change. Simultaneously holding a desire for change and a full acceptance of the present makes change possible.

Exercise: Change and Acceptance

In this exercise, each of you will first think of something you want your partner to change, then come together to discuss.

1. Allow an hour.
2. *Reflect and write*:

- What is it that you would like your partner to change?
- What is the current reality of your partner's ability in this area?
- Can you hold both an acceptance of their current limitations as well as an expectation that positive change is possible?

3. *Discuss.* In two separate dialogues of about a half hour each, you will discuss the change each of you wrote about. Pay attention to apertures and use your new dialogue skills.

WORKING AT YOUR EDGE

Yoga instructors often talk about "working at your edge"—where you are challenged just the right amount. Too little effort and you get no movement, learning, or change; too much and you'll hurt yourself or get discouraged.

One of the collaborative skills of change is learning to work at your edge. Challenging conversations that lead to growth and positive change involve helping each other take on the right amount of difficulty with an acceptance of today's limitations. You don't want to injure or discourage, but you also don't want to ask too little, of yourself or of each other, and fail to move forward.

In aperture terms, this means that in challenging conversations you are fluctuating between 5 and 10, working to keep yourself and your partner in the learning sweet spot. If your apertures are always at 10, you're not taking risks. If apertures are consistently below 5, you're likely to get hurt or discouraged.

Exercise: Working at Your Edge

Choose a topic that is challenging, but not too challenging. You are looking for the right amount that leads you into new learning without being overwhelming. You're going to experiment with working at your edge, each of you and as a couple.

1. Allow a half hour.
2. Begin your dialogue, tracking apertures as you go. Try to keep apertures between 5 and 10, hovering around 5–7 whenever possible. If you tend to push forward into conflict, you may need to sit back a bit, be patient, and allow things to unfold—more

acceptance. On the other hand, if you tend to
avoid conflict, you may need to take a few more
risks and tolerate a bit more discomfort—
more challenge.

3. *Reflect and write:*

*   How difficult was it for you to work at your edge?
*   Did you lean more toward acceptance or chal-
    lenge? Which way did your partner tend to go?
*   What did you discover about your teamwork in
    this task of creating the right balance?
*   Did you overshoot at any point and need to call a
    time-out?
*   How did remembering to balance acceptance
    with challenge help you recover open apertures?

4. *Discuss.*

THE POWER OF DECISIONS

The role of decisions in relationship improvement is often over-
looked, both by couples and therapists. I'm not sure why this
would be, since we value decisions as part of having choices in
everything from what car to buy to what time to have dinner.
Frequently in my office, after exploring an issue and concluding that a change is needed, one partner will ask, "So, how do
we change this?" I often answer that the first step is deciding
to do so. Peter Block, organizational consultant, nailed it in
the title of his book about taking action, *The Answer to How
Is Yes.*[2]

A decision is a commitment, and commitment confers
many advantages to any undertaking. Cultural commentator
David Brooks says, "Character . . . is built externally by making

commitments."[3] When we commit to something, we enter a kind of dialogue with life. We assume that there is a way forward; we engage with the task and the questions it raises, and we move forward, finding new paths we didn't know and could not know prior to deciding. Commitment means we close the option of turning around and giving up. The big commitment to a person and a relationship is realized by a myriad of smaller decisions.

Exercise: Decisions

In this exercise, you're going to decide to pursue an aspect of your vision (page 230).

1. You are going to dialogue for a half hour.
2. With written copies of your visions in hand, choose something that is in both your visions. For example, perhaps you both said that you want to support each other's dreams.
3. Discuss what it would mean to decide, commit to, and realize this aspect of your vision. Prompts for this dialogue:

- What are you each currently doing that is consistent with this aspect of your vision? Be sure to discuss each of your perspectives on this.
- What do you each see about how your own behavior could be more helpful in realizing this?
- What do you see about how your partner's behavior could be more helpful in realizing this?
- What gets in the way of being more successful?

- What do you each need to learn or change to more successfully pursue this goal?
- Do you feel ready to decide to go for this change?

4. *Reflect and write:*

- What did you like about this dialogue?
- What could have been better?
- How did you do with aperture awareness?
- What needs to happen next?

5. *Discuss.*

THE IMPORTANCE OF SIMULTANEITY

Harnessing the power of simultaneity gives you a big advantage for change, especially in a downward spiral. One source of discouragement in couples trying to reverse a downward spiral is asynchrony of efforts. If one person is trying to change, but their partner is not yet ready, the chance of success is significantly diminished.

Imagine that one afternoon, feeling distressed and discouraged about your relationship, you go for a walk. For the first part of your walk, you're sad, angry, frustrated. Then something shifts. You realize that you're in this for the long haul, and that the only reasonable thing to do is to try to sort things out and make it better. On the way home, you think about what you can do to improve the relationship. You remember your partner's frustration with your lack of appreciation and positive comments about his contributions. You decide to try to change your behavior.

As you reach the house, you see him up on a ladder, cleaning the rain gutters. You call out, "Thanks so much for taking care of that; it really needed attention." He, in the downward spiral of negative assumptions, and not realizing you are trying something new, responds defensively with "What do you mean? I did it only a few months ago!" Hurt, but trying hard to get on a new page, you ignore his rebuff.

Later, while cooking dinner you try again. "I noticed that you got asparagus. I love asparagus. Thanks." He, still in downward motion, simply says gruffly, "Whatever." For most people, it won't take but one or two more of these failed solo attempts to break your good resolve. Soon you will snap back angrily, something like "Look, I'm trying to make things better, but you, as usual, are being impossible!"

Often what happens next is a repeat of this cycle in reverse. You have used up your fragile goodwill. Your partner, reflecting on the possibility that you really are trying and that he too wants things to be better, decides to try harder. Now he is making an effort, but you're in the discouragement and anger mode and unaware of, or unresponsive to, his efforts. Then he gets discouraged. Soon you both, once again, are feeling hopeless.

Although it's important to be willing to do everything you can to contribute to a good relationship, sometimes it may be best to wait until you are both ready at the same time and agree to make a concerted effort.

THE IMPORTANCE OF NON-SIMULTANEITY

Rules are proved by their exceptions, and there are some exceptions to the rule of simultaneity. Sometimes it's possible to go first, attempt to improve your part before your partner is fully ready. Actually, in upward spirals, this happens a lot and is one of the strengths of good relationships. When there is adequate trust, people easily make unilateral contributions, whether to housework or communications. Given the demands of life, it will often be true that one of you is feeling stronger, more stable, and more loving than the other. When trust is high, it is understood that each of you will do the best you can and that sometimes one of you is stronger—in that moment.

Relationships benefit enormously when we are able to function especially well with less than desirable treatment from our partner. Couples therapist Brent Atkinson wrote, "Some of the most important interpersonal habits involve things that people must be able to do *without the help of their partners*. In fact, they must be able to do these things precisely when their partners are making it most difficult to do them. . . . The way people respond to the worst in their partners plays a central role in determining whether or not they will experience something better from them in the future."[4]

Also there is an inevitable lag in the time between your efforts to change and your partner's ability to notice. This is difficult because the person changing wants positive recognition. It helps to let your partner know when you decide to try something new. In this way, you can help reset expectations sooner in a positive direction, sometimes resulting in more teamwork and support for your efforts.

In a downward spiral it is harder, but not impossible, to move forward with unequal contributions. Be prepared to be patient and persistent or to discontinue unilateral efforts if you start to get too injured, discouraged, or concerned about fairness.

FAIRNESS

Fairness is an especially slippery slope when you are in a downward spiral and trust is low. Mammals definitely get uncomfortable when things are not fair. Researchers put two dogs side by side where they could see each other. The dogs were first trained to offer a paw for a "handshake," for which they would get a treat. The researchers then stopped giving the treat to one dog but continued with the reward for the other. Ordinarily, after a dog is trained to do a trick for a treat, when you stop giving the treat, the dog continues for a very long time to do the trick on command. But when another dog was in sight who was continuing to get the treat, the other dog stopped the behavior very quickly. No fair![5]

Perhaps even more interesting is the research with chimps showing that there is a prosocial, relationship-building aspect to our sensitivity to fairness. When two chimps are placed so that they can see each other and one is getting carrots for rewards and the other is getting grapes, the preferred treat, at some point the grape-getting chimp will stop accepting the grapes unless the other chimp is also offered grapes.[6] Related to this is the neuroscience that shows that our brains actually activate a larger reward response for giving than for receiving.[7] It is not only more blessed to give than to receive; it also feels better!

Except in a downward spiral, when we are not very prosocial and inclined to feel treated unfairly. So, how do you know when to do what you can unilaterally, or when to wait for simultaneity? Remember that putting the relationship first means understanding what best serves the relationship. This means that if going first at a time when your partner can't reciprocate costs you too dearly—in terms of your own morale, goodwill, and sense of fairness—then the cost is too high, not just for you individually but also for the relationship. Anything that compromises your ability to be a good teammate is not a win for the relationship.

On the other hand, perhaps waiting for simultaneity is seriously getting in the way of moving forward, and you feel willing and able to work to improve your side of things. Then maybe this is a time when you can move ahead unilaterally.

CHAPTER 13

Becoming Learning Partners

Your relationship can be a powerful force for change. Neuroscience tells us that neural plasticity and learning are enhanced in positive, attuned relationships.[1]

One of the most important things couples can do is to participate well in each other's changes, to become *learning partners.*

Because of our interconnectedness, we profoundly influence each other for better or worse. In *A General Theory of Love,* Thomas Lewis, Fari Amini, and Richard Lannon put it this way: "In a relationship one mind revises another; one heart changes its partner. This astounding legacy of our combined status as mammals and neural beings is *limbic revision:* the power to remodel the emotional parts of the people we love. Who we are and who we become depends in part on whom we love."[2] We have the ability to help each other heal old wounds and become better at loving each other!

The influence we have on each other is intensified in

couples by their investment and the sheer number of hours they spend with each other. In the early days of my practice, I worked with individuals. I began to realize that they were spending an hour or two with me each week to attempt certain changes, then going home to spend many times that number of hours with their partner. What if those hours could be harnessed in the service of positive changes? I turned to working with couples because a couple can build a powerful collaboration for change.

A SYSTEMIC UNDERSTANDING OF PROBLEMS

The most important part of solving problems is understanding what the problem is, and couples' problems are best understood in the context of their interconnectedness. As human beings we are designed for interconnection and interdependence. Human infants are dependent upon others for survival far longer than any other creature. During this protracted period of dependency, our nervous systems are shaped for connection of all kinds. Our limbic systems develop to tune in to others' states. Our various physiologic systems become wired in such a way that we regulate each other.

Because of this interconnectivity, people who spend time together form systems of interactions. To change behaviors that are problematic, you must understand them as interactions. Often, I hear couples arguing about who is to blame for an aspect of the relationship. Or one person is extremely angry at the other for a particular behavior, without realizing that this behavior exists in the context of interaction. Your problems and their solutions are all co-creations.

Example: Ram and Sid love going to the beach together. Ram is great at getting the picnic together, which leaves Sid free to study the map and figure out how to get to a new beach they want to explore. This collaboration works great. Now, let's add a couple of kids to the mix.

Ram and Sid still love the beach, but increasingly Sid is terrible at finding the route, gets cranky during the drive, and they arrive late and in a fight. Ram complains about the crankiness. Sid tries very hard not to be cranky, but the behavior gets worse. Finally, one day they sit down to talk about it. After a couple of false starts, they discover the pattern.

In order to put together the picnic, Ram has left Sid to get the kids ready and keep them happy in the hour leading up to getting in the car. This leaves Sid with no time to study the map, but being the super parent that he is, he has soldiered on, trying to do a great job of navigation with no preparation. The kids are happy, having been well entertained before the drive. Ram is happy, having gotten to make a great lunch. Everyone wonders why Sid is such a grouch! Once they figure this out, both feel relieved and creative problem-solving ensues.

The power to change what you do not like, in your partner or in the relationship, starts with your ability to entertain this hypothesis: *The difficulty is the result of an interaction.* This means that even when it seems like the difficulty is caused solely by your partner, you look beyond this. You question the "seemingness" of this reality and ask, *What is my participation in this problem? How is this difficulty the result of an interaction?*

I can almost guarantee you will never start with this awareness. You'll start with knowing that your partner is doing something that you don't like. It will seem practically impossible that you have a role in this. Which is why being able to approach the problem by assuming, against all you feel, that you probably are implicated is important. If you don't go looking for it, you will likely get bogged down in the effort to convince your partner of their culpability. Yes, there are occasional exceptions to this, but I assure you they are rare. Place your bets on the idea that you are dealing with a complicated, mostly unseen, interaction. Then go searching for it together.

Exercise: Discovering the Interactive Patterns

In this exercise, you are going to work together to discover the interactive pattern behind something one of you does not like. Often, when discussing a behavior you don't like in your partner, they will get defensive. Apertures start to close. Reassure them of your interest in understanding the problem as an interaction. Much light can be shed if each of you looks for the grain of truth (page 132) in your different perceptions of what is going on.

1. Spend a half hour to an hour in this dialogue.
2. Pick a problematic behavior, perhaps something you have already talked about, likely argued about. Now work together to discover what each of you is doing that makes this behavior likely or makes changing it harder.

   What is the problematic behavior you're investigating (yours or your partner's)? _____

- Are there behaviors of the other partner that typically precede or follow this behavior?
- Is there some way that these make the problem behavior more likely?
- What are the feelings or beliefs of each of you about the problem behavior?
- Is there some way that these make the problem

behavior more likely?
* Based on your exploration, what is your hypothesis about the interactive pattern?
* How might you collaborate for change?

3. *Reflect and write.*
4. *Discuss.*

THE ARC OF CHANGE

Most of our processing of information goes on outside our awareness. Psychologist Timothy Wilson notes that the brain can absorb about eleven million pieces of information a second, of which it can only process about forty consciously.[3] The brain handles the rest outside our awareness. In addition to most of our information processing being unconscious, most of our behaviors are unconscious and many serve us quite well without our conscious awareness.

But when we want to make changes, we must bring unconscious behaviors into conscious awareness, like shining a light on them. We then work toward whatever change we desire, and having achieved the change, the new behavior then goes back to being unconscious, making way for some other priority to take the stage of conscious observation.[4] The arc of change is thus:

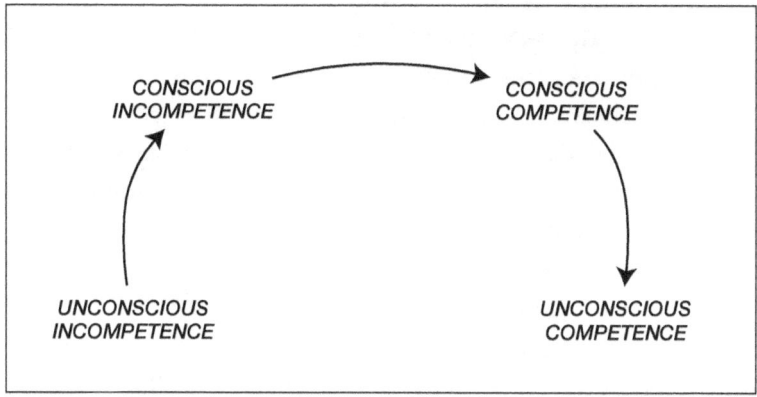

Figure 9: The Arc of Change

Now, let's look at this arc of change in terms of your collaboration as learning partners. We will explore the art of benefiting from your partner's awareness of your unconscious behaviors and how the two of you collaborate to change behaviors that are not serving the relationship. For the sake of this discussion, we are going to look at how you work together for a change in *one* of you. But, as discussed, it's also important to understand and address the interactive aspect.

Benefiting from Your Partner's Awareness

In my favorite moment of an old video of Carl Jung, the other father of modern Western psychology, Dr. Jung says, in his thick Swiss accent, something to the effect of: "You know, the thing about the unconscious is, it *really is* unconscious!"[5] I think what he meant to emphasize is that whatever it is that is unconscious is not available to us. We cannot know it, comment on it, or think about it with our conscious mind. An extremely frustrating predicament!

Our own behaviors, thoughts, and feelings are going on, sometimes without our conscious awareness. We are wary of and intimidated by this. We find it so disconcerting that we want to deny the very existence of the unconscious. This denial compounds the already-significant difficulties in changing.

Then there is the added unsettling complexity that some of what is invisible to us about ourselves is visible to others, especially those closest to us. Daniel Dennett, philosopher and cognitive psychologist, wrote, "Not only are minds accessible to outsiders; some mental activities are more accessible to outsiders than to the very 'owners' of those minds!"[6]

One morning, my three-year-old popped off with a spontaneous little song: "I can see you. I can see you. But you can't see you!" He had captured one of the odd difficulties, and potential benefits, of relationships. This is a source of misery if we cannot figure out how to work with it; a superpower for change if we can. Daniel Kahneman emphasizes that our ability to think better is related to our ability to criticize each other's thinking.[7]

It is very uncomfortable and threatening to have others see things in us that we cannot see, especially so for things we or they dislike. But if we can trust our partner enough to take seriously their observations of things outside our awareness, then we expand our ability to know ourselves and our ability to change. As Yongey Mingyur Rinpoche said, "Ultimately, happiness comes down to choosing between the discomfort of becoming aware of your mental afflictions and the discomfort of being ruled by them."[8]

When you put the relationship first, you each keep an eye on what's needed to make the relationship better. When your partner's behavior is damaging the relationship, it's your responsibility to speak to them about it.

I recently helped Nora tell Avi that she could not deal with his temper. Avi genuinely had no idea what she was talking about. He considered himself to be a reasonable and loving man and had worked hard not to be like his father, who had been very angry and sometimes violent. Avi was incredulous that Nora felt he was anything like that. Sometimes the person presenting the problem is equally incredulous: *How could you not know that your anger is a problem?!* The challenge, then, for Nora, was to draw Avi's attention to behaviors she didn't like—behaviors he himself disapproved of and was often unaware of—in a way that helped him stay open.

It's unrealistic to expect that on the first pass your partner will be persuaded that what you are describing exists and causes problems. They will most likely react with denial and disbelief, possibly getting upset. If you want more than frustration out of this process, and if the change you want seems important, then you should be prepared to be both patient and persistent. Staying connected to your alignment with, and responsibility for, the relationship is helpful. This is an example of a time when putting the relationship first does not mean putting your partner's *comfort,* or your own, first.

Your responsibility to the relationship also includes being open to dialogue about your concerns. You know what you are experiencing. You do not know everything you need to know about what is going on. For this, you need teamwork. You're asking your partner, and offering yourself, to be open to exploring and understanding.

The process of change has two phases. In Phase 1 the two of you are discussing and investigating a possible change. In Phase 2 you are collaborating to make this change a reality. The tasks of each of you are different in the two phases.

In Phase 1, the task of the partner being asked to change (the *changing partner*) is to openly consider that some (likely unconscious) behavior is a problem. The task of the other partner (the *assisting partner*) is skillful, patient presentation of their concerns and continued open exploration.

Phase 2 begins when the changing partner consciously recognizes and agrees about the problem and begins efforts to replace the problematic behavior with new desired behavior. The task of the assisting partner in Phase 2 shifts from presenting the problem to supporting change efforts.

Phases of the Arc of Change: Phase 1

In Phase 1, you discuss the assisting partner's concerns and agree to a period of investigation. Notice how this relates to "Offering to Investigate" and "Offering to Try to Understand" (pages 136 and 138).

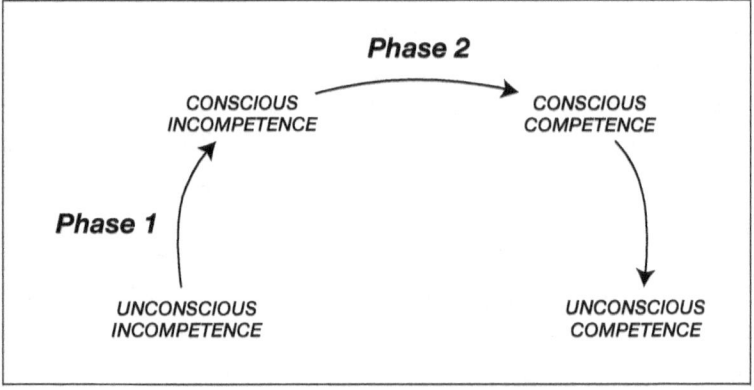

Figure 10: Arc of Change, Phases 1 and 2

At the end of the conversation between Nora and Avi, Avi turned to me in despair and said, "I don't know what to do. I really don't think she's right or that my temper is a problem. I can't agree just to make her happy." My suggestion to him was that he doesn't need to agree that she is right. He can simply agree to look into the possibility that she is onto something. Nora also needs to agree to continue to investigate.

During this investigation phase there were several times when Avi became angry and aggressive but seemed not to notice. Some of these times Nora pointed this out. Sometimes she let it go but then circled back a few days later for another discussion about his temper, mentioning the times that he had recently been angry and aggressive. This process went on for a few weeks. Sometimes they got impatient with each other. Both had to remember their agreement to investigate the problem.

When the behavior goes from being unconscious to conscious it becomes possible to discuss each partner's experience, and whether to try to change it. (For the purposes of this discussion, we'll look at teamwork when the changing partner becomes aware of the behavior and concludes that their partner's observations are valid. Of course, that is not the only possible outcome of exploration.)

There came a point when Avi started noticing how often he flew off the handle. A couple of times he stopped himself and asked Nora if this was what she was talking about. They were then able to discuss their experiences of these moments. Avi talked about how frustrated he gets—sometimes with Nora, sometimes with other things. He remembered how he felt when his dad lost his temper. Nora said that was similar to what she felt with Avi and his anger. They both agreed that, though Avi's anger was far less destructive than his father's, it was causing problems. Aggressive behaviors, they agreed, were destructive to their relationship and their goal to have a peaceful home. Avi agreed to change his behavior. Now they're ready for Phase 2, which follows after these exercises.

Exercise: Discussion of Problematic Behavior

Each of you is to identify a behavior that you wish the other to change, preferably a small one for the purposes of practicing new skills and awareness. This needs to be a behavior that your partner is unaware of or only partially aware of. On two separate occasions you are going to dialogue about each of these behaviors for a half hour, or until you reach agreement to investigate the behavior.

1. The assisting partner begins a dialogue about what behavior they observe and its effect on them, or why they wish their partner to change this.
2. The potentially changing partner's job is to listen and, at some point, agree to study the problem, to try to notice this behavior. You can discuss whether you want reminders, and if so in what form.
3. Remember that the goal is not to agree with your partner if you don't, but to agree to investigate.
4. Agree on when you will next check in about your observations. You now begin the period of observation.
5. Record the following:

     Date _____
     Assisting partner _____
     Changing partner _____
     Problematic unconscious behavior, according to assisting partner _____

6. *Reflect and write.*
7. *Discuss.*

Exercise: Discussion of Desired Change

When the partner being asked to change feels that they have been able to observe the behavior, share your observations with each other and then discuss changes.

1. Discuss your observations about the behavior, including any differences in how you experience it.
2. Discuss willingness to change on the part of the partner being asked to change. If they are not willing to change this behavior, you begin again with discussion of a different problematic behavior.
3. If there is willingness to change, discuss what the change will be.
4. Record the following:

   Date _____
   Assisting partner _____
   Changing partner _____
   Problematic unconscious behavior, according to assisting partner _____
   Date of conscious awareness by changing partner _____
   Date of agreement to change _____
   Description of the agreed-upon change _____
   _____

5. *Reflect and write.*
6. *Discuss.*

Phases of the Arc of Change: Phase 2

Phase 2 begins when there is conscious recognition and acceptance of the problem and agreement to change. Now, the task of the changing partner is to replace the problematic behavior with the new desired behavior. The task of the assisting partner in Phase 2 is to support change efforts.

There are problems of commission and of omission. In other words, sometimes something is being *done* that's not helpful, and other times the *absence* of a helpful behavior is the problem. In Avi's case he's doing something—getting aggressive and unpleasant when he's angry. Not coming home on time for dinner is an example of the absence of a behavior that would benefit the relationship.

In Phase 2 the changing partner first inhibits the old behavior, then replaces it with the new. This means that even though you don't know yet what the new behavior is or how to do it, you simply don't allow yourself to do the old behavior. Once Avi agreed to stop expressing his anger aggressively, his first task was to learn to notice his anger and not react aggressively. (See "Mindfulness, Containment, and Response Flexibility" on page 168.)

When the problem is the absence of a behavior (omission), the changing partner is to learn more about the situations in which the desired behavior is missing. In the example of not showing up on time for dinner, the changing partner becomes more aware of time as they rush to try to finish work before leaving for home—and of how this is the setup for not getting home in time.

Finally the changing partner practices new behavior. Avi, for example, might experiment when he gets angry with taking a time-out to observe his reaction and let himself calm down. The late-for-dinner partner learns to stop working in time to get home for dinner and, when not possible, to call to say when they will be there.

In Phase 2, the task of the assisting partner changes. They stop calling attention to the old behavior (which, of course, will take some time to change), and instead express appreciation for any successful inhibition of the old behavior or shift toward the new behavior. One of the most common mistakes during a change process is that the assisting partner fails to make this shift. The changing partner no longer needs to be told they are doing this annoying thing. Reminders will be experienced as demeaning or as a lack of confidence in their efforts, frustrating them and impeding their progress. For most people in the assisting role, this is a welcome change once they get the hang of it. Now, instead of being the bearer of bad tidings and confrontation, they are the source of positive acknowledgment and appreciation.

Changing behaviors will likely trigger emotional reactions in both partners. The behaviors your partner wants you to change are often ways you've developed to feel safe and comfortable. As you inhibit them, and then replace them with new behaviors, you're likely to feel vulnerable, insecure, awkward, resentful, or other uncomfortable emotions. With mindful awareness and compassionate interest in your reactions, you'll learn more about yourself. This learning is part of your success and will make you stronger and more resilient.

The changes may also bring up emotional reactions in the assisting partner. A common early reaction to your partner making changes you've requested is to feel an *increase* in feelings of anger, frustration, or despair. This will seem paradoxical to both of you. After all, you're finally getting what you wanted, right?

Often when relief from discomfort is in sight, our coping mechanisms shift from minimizing awareness, when change seemed impossible, to a fuller awareness of our distress. It is important that both of you understand this as a normal part of the change process and not take it as a signal that something is wrong. This is a stay-the-course moment. The assisting partner can protect their partner's morale by being judicious about when and how they share these feelings. The changing partner can exercise patience with this reaction, and not let it distract from the task at hand. With time, this reaction will run its course and be replaced by feelings of relief and appreciation.

THE IMPORTANCE OF RECOGNIZING
EARLY CHANGE

An underappreciated aspect of the change process is that the first 2 percent of the change requires about 80 percent of the total effort needed for that change. These changes are not linear. Turning the corner is often the hardest part. The change that follows will likely be easier and more apparent. Not understanding this, you may feel discouraged about lack of progress at exactly the point you should be celebrating the momentous 2 percent.

This can be especially challenging for the assisting partner. Often the change is something that you have been requesting for a long time. You've grown exasperated with the behavior and perhaps pessimistic about the possibility your partner will ever change. You feel you need dramatic evidence that what you want is possible and that your partner is really trying. You may look at a 2 percent shift, compare it to what you really want, and feel this is further evidence that change is impossible. This puny effect is hardly what you'd hoped for! It's easy at this point to assume, mistakenly, that the effort behind the puny effect was also puny.

Meanwhile, your partner has been exerting enormous effort to get this initial 2 percent change. Failure to appreciate and support early change, or worse to resume criticism and confrontation, is like trampling a seedling, possibly sending you both back into hopelessness. Being good learning partners means you each learn to recognize and celebrate any initial change in the right direction, no matter how small.

Exercise: Phase 2

Based on the discussion and change agreed upon from the previous exercises, you proceed to Phase 2.

1. The changing partner first inhibits the old behavior or becomes aware of the absence of a wanted behavior.
2. They then begin the new behavior.
3. The assisting partner ignores instances of the old behavior (or lack of wanted behavior) and is overtly appreciative of both effort and success. It's also helpful in the early stages for the changing partner to reassure the assisting partner of ongoing efforts.
4. When change occurs, it's important that you each note it and then appreciate each other for this successful teamwork. Celebrate!
5. *Reflect and write:*

   • Your role (change or assist) _____
   • Date progress toward change first noted _____
   • How did you celebrate?
   • Date when new behavior is happening more than 50 percent of the time _____
   • How did you celebrate?
   • Other observations?

6. *Discuss.*

THE JOURNEY: COMMITMENT, ENDURANCE, SKILLFUL TEAMWORK

Successfully implementing change doesn't mean you will never slip up or revert to old behavior. It does mean that at such moments you stay alert and mindful to learn as much as you can about what sets you up for success or failure. If you find yourself waffling—sometimes paying attention, sometimes not—you may need to revisit your motivation. Are you having mixed feelings about making this change? What is in the way of you making a concerted, 100 percent change effort? This may be a moment to review:

- Are you holding the *possibility* that you and your partner can change?
- Are you staying connected to your *vision* as something you are *learning to do*?
- Are you including *acceptance* as part of change?
- Are you using the power of *decisions* and *commitment*?
- Are you working *at your edge*?
- Are you understanding your *difficulties* and *learning* as co-productions?
- Are you doing the *right experiment*—helping your partner to be their best self?

Being part of a loving couple is not a goal you accomplish; it's a journey. Using aperture awareness, mindfulness, and dialogue, you can engage together in the adventure of turning problems into learning to create connection and joy.

CONCLUSION

The Poetry of Relationship

We love a riddle that, with just the right amount of effort, we can solve. But we sometimes hate the gigantic, never fully solvable, ongoing riddle of life and relationship. Deconstruction of the complexities of relationship, finding the small solvable riddles hidden in the larger riddle, can be helpful. In this book we have, at times, taken the relationship watch or toaster apart to learn of the pieces and how they fit together—what makes it tick or toast. But in the end, a relationship is not a watch or a toaster. Watches and toasters perform simple, reliable functions, and when they don't, we can fix them or replace them. When we expect relationships to be more like watches and toasters than poems, they don't make sense.

Poet Jane Hirshfield in *Ten Windows* compares true poems to true loves. Poems, she says, have a "sense of uncontainable and mysterious surplus . . . A poem is a cup of words filled past its brim, carrying meanings beyond its own measurable capacity."[1] This aspect of poems and relationships is so very different from the watch and the toaster and the reductionist, scientific world of specificity and precision.

Physics has long grappled with the quantum nature of reality where light is both particle and wave and Schrödinger's cat is both dead and alive. When we find a way to get comfortable with paradox and the unknown, to make friends with conflict and contradiction, we enter the bounty of the "uncontainable and mysterious surplus," the very real world of infinite possibilities where relationship, like poetry, "draws from us what we did not know was there to be drawn."[2]

The frustrations of relationship are less maddening when we remember to appreciate that inspiration and delight are at times inseparable from being confounded and mystified. "Good poems make clear without making simple."[3]

Hirshfield also says:

> Poetry's ends are, in truth, peculiar, viewed from the byways of ordinary speech. But it is this oddness that makes poems so needed— true poems, like true love, undo us and un-island. Contrary, sensual, subversive, they elude our customary allegiance to surface reality, purpose, and will. A good poem is comprehensive and thirsty. It pulls toward what is invisible to an overly directed looking. . . . Poems rummage the drawers of what does not yet exist but might, in the world, in us. . . . A good poem reveals, entering and leaving altered whatever it meets.[4]

Here's what I would say about relationships, using Hirshfield's words:

Some of *relationship's* ends are, in truth, peculiar when viewed from the byways of *ordinary life*. But it is this oddness that makes *relationships* so needed—*important relationships* undo us and un-island. Contrary, sensual, subversive, they elude our customary allegiance to surface reality, purpose, and will. A good *relationship* is comprehensive and thirsty. It pulls toward what is invisible to an overly directed looking. . . . *Relationships* rummage the drawers of what does not yet exist but might, in the world, in us. . . . A good *relationship* reveals, entering and leaving altered whatever it meets.

And herein lie the difficulties. You may want to be un-islanded, less lonely. But do you want to be undone? You probably like being under the influence of the sensual, but what about the contrary and subversive? How do you feel when pulled toward the invisible? Or when your relationship is thirsty and rummaging your drawers? What about when it reveals your hiding places? And do you really want to be altered?

Hirshfield also says, "A good poem is a through-passage, words that leave poet, reader, and themselves ineradicably changed. Having read a poem that matters, the person who holds the page is different than he or she was before."[5]

A good *relationship* is a through-passage that leaves you ineradicably changed. Having a relationship that matters, you are different than you were before. Relationships, like poems, transform us. This can be unnerving. Our attachment to being "me" resists this transformation. Yet if we can surrender to it, we discover that we are still ourselves, only larger. We learn to trust that life, especially in relationship, offers growth and expansion, and that part of our essence is this ability to be transformed.

Poems and relationships are alchemical vessels. They are the means by which we realize, and participate in, the transformational, the transcendent. As such, they have the power to inspire and delight as well as to confound and mystify. We rarely complain of inspiration and delight. But when relationships confound and mystify, we can get very uncomfortable.

"Poems search for transformations not least by seeking beauty."[6] Follow beauty and it will lead you soon into chaos and then back again to beauty. Follow love and it will do the same. Let it surprise you, amuse you, disrupt you, redeem you. It will show you (the best and worst of) who you are.

"Poetry's leaps, images, stories, and metaphors are the oxygen possibility breathes."[7] Relationship's leaps, images, stories, and metaphors are the oxygen possibility breathes. Don't be afraid of those moments when your partner makes a leap you cannot follow. Open wide to their story, especially when it is not yours. Make room, lots of room, for possibility.

Expect poetry in your relationship and you will not be disappointed. Expect to be stirred and disturbed, with no words to describe what is happening to you. Expect to feel that something magnificent is being held just out of reach. Expect to feel frustrated, confused, and lost. Expect beauty, chaos, and delight, with much peering into darkness.

Be brave enough to flounder in the mystery of life, together. Say what you can, especially when it doesn't make sense, and then listen as the words resound into silence. Keep each other good company while you wait for wisdom to arrive. Reward amply the courage to be lost while looking for more understanding and more love than you yet have.

May your life together be full.

Acknowledgments

I am deeply grateful to my clients and students for the privilege of working with them as they courageously explore this trackless land of learning and love. This book has grown out of those explorations. Thank you so much for all I have learned from you.

For all the wonderful and difficult hours of instruction and silence, I am grateful to Spirit Rock Meditation Center, Barre Center for Buddhist Studies (Insight Meditation Society), teachers Thich Nhat Hanh, Adyashanti, Bhikkhu Analayo, and a host of other teachers and fellow students. Thank you all for your practice and for helping me with mine.

A special thanks to Emilie Conrad and Larry Hatlett for their inspired teaching of the wisdom of the body, deeply with me still.

I have been nurtured and taught by caring and talented therapists. In particular Abe Levitsky widened the territory to include studies of consciousness itself. David Willingham helped me to replace fear with love. I remember each with deepest gratitude.

I've had the good fortune of working with colleagues devoted to compassionate investigation and teaching in the mysterious realms of human hearts and minds. Among the first to open these doors for me were Irv Yalom and David Spiegel in the Department of Psychiatry and Behavioral Sciences at Stanford School of Medicine, and Nathan Epstein, chairman of the Department of Psychiatry and Human Behavior at the Warren Alpert Medical School of Brown University. Deepest gratitude.

My work with and understanding of couples have been nourished by the contributions of so many that have come before me. John and Julie Gottman, Esther Perel, Susan Johnson, Terry Real, Stan Tatkin, Ellyn Bader, and Peter Pearson, to name just a few, have helped take couples therapy from an afterthought to a flourishing field of discovery.

My interest in and understanding of the neuroscience of relationships, the intersection with mindfulness, and the art of dialogue have been furthered by Fari Amini, Brent Atkinson, Sharon Begley, Louis Cozolino, Richard Davidson, Norman Doidge, Daniel Goleman, Marco Iacoboni, William Isaacs, Michael Kahn, Richard Lannon, Joseph LeDoux, Thomas Lewis, David Rock, and Daniel Siegel. Thanks to all of you and so many others for your work and writing in these areas.

Stanford Continuing Studies has given me invaluable opportunities to teach and develop my work. It has been a pleasure to work with such a well-run and inspiring organization. Thank you.

A special heartfelt thanks to Jane Hirshfield for her books and poetry and for generously allowing me to use her wise and beautiful words in the conclusion of this book.

So many friends and colleagues have steadfastly supported me and the creation of this book, contributing encouragement, editing, ideas, guidance, and more. Thank you, Sam Douglas, for your careful and extensive edits early on and for seeing the potential in this book; Michael Tushman and Marjorie Williams, for your friendship, encouragement, editing, and advice; Mariquita West, friend, colleague, passionate writer and reader, wise and loving human being. Thanks also to Beth Grossman, Carina Sammartino, Naomi Andrews and Dan Levin, Strat Sherman, Meredith Davis, John Seely Brown,

Andrea Vinley Converse, Nick Dela Cruz, Eric FitzMedrud, Lynn and Julian Gorodsky, Jean Kirsch, Florence and Alan Kraut, Meri Mitsuyoshi, Rachael Neumann, Edward Siegel, Julia Wenegrat, and Pippa White, for support, advice, and friendship.

Collaboration with Girl Friday Productions to publish this book has been a gift and a pleasure. Many people there have contributed enormously to producing this book. In particular, Emilie Sandoz-Voyer has been an energetic, wise, and creative partner. I appreciate so much her diligence in getting to know and understand this book and me. Thank you all so much.

I'm grateful to have had a family devoted to learning, especially about relationships. Special thanks to my sister, Linda Ford, for all your wisdom and love. And to my late parents, Dennis and Lanelle Ford, who taught me that life is learning and that people are the most worthwhile of mysteries.

I am constantly moved by the creativity and wisdom of our children, Tory, Jonah, Zoe, and son-in-law Sam. Their loving and generous support—especially our raucous brainstorming sessions—has been invaluable. They have inspired me, taught me, and been patient with me as I learned how to become a better human being. Most especially, thanks for all the music!

Sharing life and love with Peter Finkelstein—friend, husband, colleague, and life partner—is completely inseparable from every aspect of this book, and my life. Peter's unshakable belief in relationships and in learning is extraordinary. Additionally, his passion for books and language has fueled the creation of this book and filled our lives with joy. Thank you for believing in me in every way and supporting my work, with your creativity, honest criticism, and generous praise.

APPENDIX A

What About Sex?

In this book I do not talk directly about sex. Given how important sex is in many couples' relationships, I want to say a few things about this choice.

There are aspects of a couple's erotic relationship that are the same as, intertwined with, and inextricable from everything else in the relationship. Using this book to work on your relationship will likely have an impact on this part of your life. In fact, everything in the book can be applied to your sexual relationship. In their erotic lives, couples have physical and verbal dialogues, and benefit from mindfulness, learning, and change. You can definitely use this book as a guide to improving your sexual relationship. As you work with the ideas and exercises in the book, you may find it useful to consider how they relate to your erotic life with your partner. And yet there are some things, many things, about sex that deserve specific attention. I have decided not to attempt that here.

That said, let me try to anticipate a few of your questions.

Improving your relationship in general will often contribute to having a better sex life, but not always. Working on and improving your sex life will often improve your relationship in general, but not always. There are therapists who specialize in sexual problems; the good ones also understand the importance of the rest of the relationship and how to work with it. Likewise, good couples therapists are able to include your sexuality as part of what they are helping you with.

Here are a few good books about sex:

- Eric FitzMedrud, *The Better Man* (Wonderwell, 2023)
- Ian Kerner, *She Comes First* (William Morrow, 2016)
- Emily Nagoski, *Come as You Are* (Simon & Schuster, 2015)
- Esther Perel, *Mating in Captivity* (Harper, 2006)

APPENDIX B

Mindfulness Resources

Guided Meditations

- Martin Boroson, teaching one-moment meditation in an excellent short video: https://www .youtube.com/watch?v=YiC8ktpev30&t=2s
- Adyashanti, "Sitting in Stillness," in the Waking Up app by Sam Harris, available in the App Store
- Bhikkhu Analayo: https://www.buddhistinquiry. org/resources/breathing-audio/
- Thich Nhat Hanh, "Calm-Ease," Plum Village App, available in the App Store, or via YouTube

Places to Learn Mindfulness

- Mindfulness Based Stress Reduction: There are now many courses in MBSR, as originally developed by Jon Kabat-Zinn; you may find them at

your local health-care facility or university and through other community resources.
- Spirit Rock Meditation Center, Woodacre, California
- Barre Center for Buddhist Studies and Insight Meditation Society, Barre, Massachusetts
- Yoga classes: There are now many kinds of yoga classes widely available, some more like exercise/ fitness classes, others more mindfulness based. I recommend finding a class in the Iyengar tradition.

Books About Mindfulness and Buddhism

- Stephen Batchelor, *Buddhism Without Beliefs: A Contemporary Guide to Awakening* (Riverhead Books, 1997)
- Daniel Goleman and Richard J. Davidson, *Altered Traits* (Avery, 2018)
- Shauna Shapiro, *Good Morning, I Love You* (Sounds True, 2022)
- Robert Wright, *Why Buddhism Is True* (Simon & Schuster, 2017)

APPENDIX C

Image for Different Realities Exercise (Page 87)

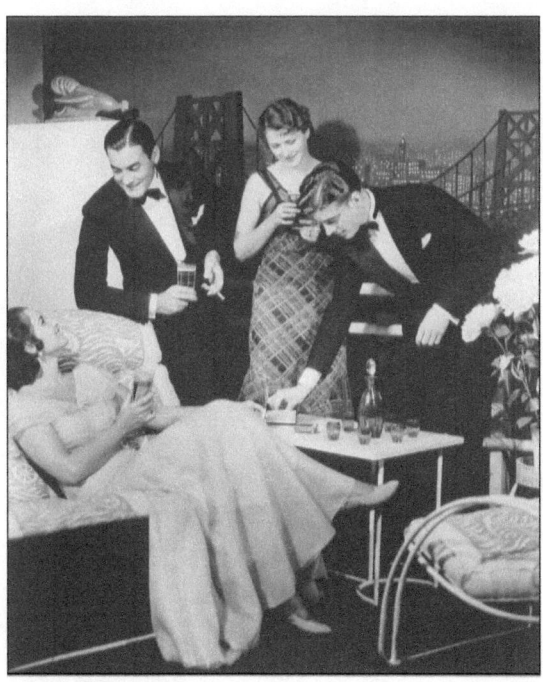

Credit: iStock, George Marks

Notes

INTRODUCTION

1   Charles Brenner, "Brief Communication: Evenly Hovering Attention," *Psychoanalytic Quarterly* 69, no. 3 (2000): 545–49, doi:10.1002/j.2167-4086.2000.tb00574.x.

2   James S. Grotstein, "Notes on Bion's 'Memory and Desire,'" *Journal of the American Academy of Psychoanalysis* 28, no. 4 (2000): 687–94.

3   University of Toronto, "Discovery Shows How Brain 'Fills in Blanks' to Help Us See," *ScienceDaily*, June 2, 2000, www .sciencedaily.com/releases/2000/06/000601164617.htm.

4   Susan M. Johnson, Brent Bradley, James L. Furrow, Alison Lee, Gail Palmer, Doug Tilley et al., *Becoming an Emotionally Focused Couple Therapist: The Workbook* (Routledge, 2005), 41.

5   Harry Stack Sullivan and Helen Swick Perry, *The Interpersonal Theory of Psychiatry* (Norton, 1974), 10.

PART ONE: APERTURE AND APERTURE AWARENESS

1   George E. Vaillant, *Triumphs of Experience* (Belknap Press of Harvard University Press, 2012), 50.

CHAPTER 1: WHAT IS APERTURE?

1   F. B. M. de Waal, *Mama's Last Hug: Animal Emotions and What They Tell Us About Ourselves* (Norton, 2019), 90.

2   Source unknown.

3   Louis J. Cozolino, *The Neuroscience of Human Relationships:*

Attachment and the Developing Social Brain (Norton, 2006), 115–16; H. E. Fisher, "Lust, Attraction, and Attachment in Mammalian Reproduction," *Human Nature* 9 (1998): 23–52, https://link.springer.com/article/10.1007/s12110 -998-1010-5#:~:text=This%20paper%20proposes%20that%20 mammals,mates%2C%20accompanied%20in%20humans%20 by; H. E. Fisher, *Why We Love: The Nature and Chemistry of Romantic Love* (Holt, 2004).

4   Thomas Lewis, Fari Amini, and Richard Lannon, *A General Theory of Love* (Random House, 2000), 84–86.

5   Andrea M. Schultz, Samantha M. Chao, and J. Michael McGinnis, *Integrative Medicine and the Health of the Public: A Summary of the February 2009 Summit* (National Academies Press, 2009), 13–14.

6   C. A. Nelson, N. A. Fox, and C. H. Zeanah, *Romania's Abandoned Children: Deprivation, Brain Development, and the Struggle for Recovery* (Harvard University Press, 2014).

7   Mahatma Gandhi, *All Men Are Brothers: Life and Thoughts of Mahatma Gandhi as Told in His Own Words* (Literary Licensing, 2011), 136.

8   Louis J. Cozolino, *The Neuroscience of Psychotherapy: Building and Rebuilding the Human Brain* (Norton, 2002), 178.

9   Tony Kushner, *Thinking About the Longstanding Problems of Virtue and Happiness: Essays, a Play, Two Poems and a Prayer* (Nick Hern Books, 1995), 40.

10 Diana Fosha, Daniel Siegel, and Marion F. Solomon, *The Healing Power of Emotion: Affective Neuroscience, Development & Clinical Practice* (Norton, 2009), 80; E. Z. Tronick, "Emotions and Emotional Communication in Infants," *American Psychologist* no. 44 (1989): 112–19, https://psycnet.apa.org/record/1989-25649-001.

11 James A. Coan, Hillary S. Schaefer, and Richard J. Davidson, "Lending a Hand: Social Regulation of the Neural Response to Threat," *Psychological Science* 17, no. 12 (2006): 1032–39, https://doi.org/10.1111/j.1467-9280.2006.01832.x.

12 Susan M. Johnson, *Hold Me Tight: Seven Conversations for a Lifetime of Love* (Little, Brown Spark, 2008), 47.

13 Cozolino, *The Neuroscience of Psychotherapy*, 62–63.

14 Cozolino, *The Neuroscience of Human Relationships*, 64.

15 Lewis, Amini, and Lannon, *A General Theory of Love*, 60.

16 Lewis, Amini, and Lannon, *A General Theory of Love*, 62–63, 142, 144.

17 Adapted from Joseph LeDoux, *Synaptic Self: How Our Brains Become Who We Are* (Penguin Books, 2002), 123.

18 David Rock, *Your Brain at Work: Strategies for Overcoming Distraction, Regaining Focus, and Working Smarter All Day Long* (Harper Business, 2009), 105; Lewis, Amini, and Lannon, *A General Theory of Love*, 54.

19 Cozolino, *The Neuroscience of Psychotherapy*, 80–85; LeDoux, *Synaptic Self*, 122–23; Daniel Kahneman, *Thinking, Fast and Slow* (Farrar, Straus and Giroux, 2011), 25.

20 Gilbert Keith Chesterton, *The Defendant* (J. M. Dent & Sons, 1901), 106.

21 Cozolino, *The Neuroscience of Psychotherapy*, 185.

22 L. M. Coutts and F. W. Schneider, "Affiliative Conflict Theory: An Investigation of the Intimacy Equilibrium and Compensation Hypothesis," *Journal of Personality and Social Psychology* 34, no. 6 (1976): 1135–42, https://doi.org/10.1037/0022-3514.34.6.1135.

23 Cozolino, *The Neuroscience of Human Relationships*, 157, 164.

24 M. Argyle and J. Dean, "Eye-Contact, Distance, and Affiliation," *Sociometry* 28, no. 3 (1965): 289–304.

25 A. Mehrabian, "Inference of Attitudes from the Posture, Orientation, and Distance of a Communicator," *Journal of Consulting and Clinical Psychology* 32, no. 3 (1968): 296–308, https://psycnet.apa.org/doiLanding?doi=10.1037%2Fh0025906; W. T. James, "A Study of the Expression of Bodily Posture," *Journal of General Psychology* 7, no. 2 (1932): 405–37, https://www.tandfonline.com/toc/vgen20/7/2;

Argyle and Dean, "Eye-Contact, Distance, and Affiliation," 289–304, https://psycnet.apa.org/record/1965-15019-001.

CHAPTER 2: ARRIVING IN
THE PRESENT MOMENT

1   Matthew A. Killingsworth and Daniel T. Gilbert, "A Wandering Mind Is an Unhappy Mind," *Science* 330, no. 6006 (2010): 932, https://www.science.org/doi/10.1126/science.1192439.

2   William James, *The Principles of Psychology* (Holt, 1890), 124.

3   "About Jon Kabat-Zinn," Jon-Kabat-Zinn.com, accessed October 21, 2024, https://jonkabat-zinn.com/about/jon-kabat-zinn/.

4   Daniel Goleman and Richard J. Davidson, *Altered Traits* (Avery, 2018), 78, 90, 92–96, 106–12, 139, 172, 180, 196–97, 253, 257; David Rock, *Your Brain at Work: Strategies for Overcoming Distraction, Regaining Focus, and Working Smarter All Day Long* (Harper Business, 2009), 83, 91, 94–95.

5   Stephen Batchelor, *Buddhism Without Beliefs: A Contemporary Guide to Awakening* (Riverhead Books, 1997), 25.

6   Lisa Krieger, "When the Music Stops, the Brain Gets Going," *Mercury News*, August 2, 2007, https://www.mercurynews.com/2007/08/02/when-the-music-stops-the-brain-gets-going/; Sridharan et al., "Neural Dynamics of Event Segmentation in Music: Converging Evidence for Dissociable Ventral and Dorsal Networks," *Neuron* 55, no. 3 (2007): 521–32, https://www.cell.com/neuron/fulltext/S0896-6273(07)00500-4; Maggie Jackson, *Uncertain* (Prometheus Books, 2023), xxiii.

7   Rock, *Your Brain at Work*, 67.

8   William Isaacs, *Dialogue: The Art of Thinking Together* (Crown Currency, 1999), 174.

9   Daniel Kahneman, *Thinking, Fast and Slow* (Farrar, Straus and Giroux, 2011), 19–20.

CHAPTER 3: WHAT YOU CAN DO
WITH APERTURE AWARENESS

1   Thomas Lewis, Fari Amini, and Richard Lannon, *A General Theory of Love* (Random House, 2000), 205.

2   John M. Gottman and Nan Silver, *The Seven Principles for Making Marriage Work: A Practical Guide from the Country's Foremost Relationship Expert*, rev. ed. (Harmony, 2015), 328–29.

PART TWO: DIALOGUE

1   Michael D. Kahn, *The Tao of Conversation: How to Talk About Things That Really Matter, in Ways That Encourage New Ideas, Deepen Intimacy, and Build Effective and Creative Working Relationships* (New Harbinger Publications, 1995), 11.

CHAPTER 4: WHAT IS DIALOGUE?

1   Kahn, *The Tao of Conversation*, 5.

2   E. F. Loftus, *Eyewitness Testimony* (Harvard University Press, 1979); Hal Arkowitz and Scott O. Lilienfeld, "Why Science Tells Us Not to Rely on Eyewitness Accounts," *Scientific American*, January 1, 2010, https://www.scientificamerican.com/article/do-the-eyes-have-it/; Daniel Kahneman, *Thinking, Fast and Slow* (Farrar, Straus and Giroux, 2011), 1, 201; Louis J. Cozolino, *The Neuroscience of Psychotherapy: Building and Rebuilding the Human Brain* (Norton, 2002), 136–37; K. N. Dunbar and J. A. Fugelsang, "Causal Thinking in Science: How Scientists and Students Interpret the Unexpected," in M. E. Gorman, R. D. Tweney, D. C. Gooding, and A. P. Kincannon (eds.), *Scientific and Technological Thinking* (2005): 57–79, https://psycnet.apa.org/record/2004-18516-003; Maggie Jackson, *Uncertain: The Wisdom and Wonder of Being Unsure* (Prometheus, 2023), 136.

3   Loftus, *Eyewitness Testimony*; Arkowitz and Lilienfeld, "Why Science Tells Us Not to Rely on Eyewitness Accounts."

4   Dunbar and Fugelsang, "Causal Thinking in Science," 57–79.

5   Leon Festinger, *A Theory of Cognitive Dissonance* (Stanford University Press, 1957).

6   A. W. Kruglanski and D. M. Webster, "Motivated Closing of the Mind: 'Seizing' and 'Freezing,'" *Psychological Review* 103, no. 2 (1996): 263–83, https://doiorg.libproxy.scu.edu/10 .1037/0033-295X.103.2.263.

7   Cozolino, *The Neuroscience of Psychotherapy*, 135–36.

8   George E. Vaillant, *Adaptation to Life* (Little, Brown, 1977).

9   Jackson, *Uncertain*, 136.

10   Esther Perel and Mary Alice Miller, "Letters from Esther #52: A Good Question Changes the Story," https://www .estherperel.com/blog/letters-from-esther-52-a-good -question-changes-the-story.

11   Peter M. Senge, *Presence: Human Purpose and the Field of the Future* (Crown Business, 2005), 31.

12   Isaacs, *Dialogue: The Art of Thinking Together*, 5.

13   John M. Gottman and Nan Silver, *The Seven Principles for Making Marriage Work: A Practical Guide from the Country's Foremost Relationship Expert* (Harmony, 1999), 116.

14   John Keats, letter to his brothers Tom and George, 1817, https://www.poetryfoundation.org/articles/69384/selections -from-keatss-letters.

15   *Snake Talk*, live performance by Naomi Newman, Traveling Jewish Theatre, San Francisco, CA, 1989.

CHAPTER 5: CULTIVATING THE SKILLS OF DIALOGUE

1   Esther Perel and Mary Alice Miller, "Feeling Alone in a Relationship? You're Not Alone," https://www.estherperel .com/blog/feeling-alone-in-a-relationship-youre-not-alone.

2   William H. Armstrong, *Study Is Hard Work* (David R. Godine Publishing, 1995), 7.

3   D. Lee and D. Hatesohl, "Listening: Our Most Used
     Communications Skill," University of Missouri, https://
     extension2.missouri.edu/cm150.

4   David Rock, *Your Brain at Work: Strategies for Overcoming
     Distraction, Regaining Focus, and Working Smarter All Day
     Long* (Harper Business, 2009), 108–10.

5   William Isaacs, *Dialogue: The Art of Thinking Together*
     (Crown Currency, 1999), 174.

CHAPTER 6: DIFFICULTIES
WILL ARISE: STRATEGIES

1   Louis J. Cozolino, *The Neuroscience of Psychotherapy:
     Building and Rebuilding the Human Brain* (Norton, 2002),
     187–88, 229; Marco Iacoboni, *Mirroring People* (Farrar,
     Straus and Giroux, 2008), 3–6.

2   Krista Tippett, *Becoming Wise: An Inquiry into the Mystery
     and Art of Living* (Penguin Press, 2016), 120.

3   Woody Allen, *Annie Hall* (United Artists, 1977).

4   K. N. Dunbar and J. A. Fugelsang, "Causal Thinking
     in Science: How Scientists and Students Interpret the
     Unexpected," in M. E. Gorman, R. D. Tweney, D. C. Gooding,
     and A. P. Kincannon (eds.), *Scientific and Technological
     Thinking* (2005): 57–79, https://psycnet.apa.org/
     record/2004-18516-003.

5   K. Murata, "Intrusive or Co-operative? A Cross-Cultural
     Study of Interruption," *Journal of Pragmatics* 21, no. 4 (1994):
     385–400, https://psycnet.apa.org/record/1994-40939-001;
     T. Stiver, N. J. Enfield, P. Brown, C. Englert, M. Hayashi,
     T. Heinemann et al., "Universals and Cultural Variation in
     Turn-Taking in Conversation," *Proceedings of the National
     Academy of Sciences of the United States of America* 106,
     no. 26 (2009): 10587–92, www.pnas.org/cgi/doi/10.1073
     /pnas.0903616106.

6   Irvin D. Yalom, *Existential Psychotherapy* (Basic Books,
     1980), 371.

CHAPTER 7: REPAIR

1 Louis J. Cozolino, *The Neuroscience of Psychotherapy: Building and Rebuilding the Human Brain* (Norton, 2002), 193.

2 Frans de Waal, *Mama's Last Hug: Animal Emotions and What They Tell Us About Ourselves* (Norton, 2019), 135.

3 Diana Fosha, Daniel Siegel, and Marion F. Solomon, *The Healing Power of Emotion: Affective Neuroscience, Development & Clinical Practice* (Norton, 2009), 182; E. Z. Tronick, "Emotions and Emotional Communication in Infants," *American Psychologist* 44, no. 2 (1989): 112–19, https://psycnet.apa.org/record/1989-25649-001.

PART THREE: MINDFULNESS AND INTERNAL SKILLS

1 Louisa May Alcott, *Little Women*, new ed. (Floating Press, 2009), 861.

CHAPTER 8: MINDFUL AWARENESS AND EMOTIONS

1 Daniel J. Siegel, *Pocket Guide to Interpersonal Neurobiology* (Norton, 2012), 19-3, 19-4, 19-6, 19-7.

2 A. R. Damasio, *Descartes' Error: Emotion, Reason, and the Human Brain* (Grosset/Putnam, 1994); A. R. Damasio, "Emotion in the Perspective of an Integrated Nervous System," *Brain Research Reviews* 26, nos. 2–3 (1998): 83–86, https://doi.org/10.1016/S0165-0173(97)00064-7; A. R. Damasio, "Emotion and the Human Brain," in A. R. Damasio, A. Harrington, J. Kagan, B. S. McEwen, H. Moss, and R. Shaikh (eds.), *Unity of Knowledge: The Convergence of Natural and Human Science* (2001): 101–6, https://psycnet.apa.org/record/2001-01110-011.

3 Brent J. Atkinson, *Emotional Intelligence in Couples Therapy: Advances from Neurobiology and the Science of Intimate*

Relationships (Norton, 2005), 20, 24; Damasio, *Descartes' Error*; A. R. Damasio, "Emotion in the Perspective of an Integrated Nervous System," *Brain Research Reviews* 26, nos. 2–3 (1998): 83–86, https://doi.org/10.1016/S0165-0173(97)00064-7; Damasio, "Emotion and the Human Brain."

4   Daniel J. Siegel, *The Mindful Brain: Reflection and Attunement in the Cultivation of Well-Being*, 1st ed. (W. W. Norton, 2007), 42.

5   S. Schacter and J. E. Singer, "Cognitive, Social, and Physiological Determinants of Emotional State," *Psychological Review* 69 (1962): 379–99, https://psycnet.apa.org/record/1963-06064-001; J. LeDoux, *The Emotional Brain* (Simon & Schuster, 1996), 203.

6   Louis J. Cozolino, *The Neuroscience of Psychotherapy: Building and Rebuilding the Human Brain* (Norton, 2002), 102.

7   David Rock, *Your Brain at Work: Strategies for Overcoming Distraction, Regaining Focus, and Working Smarter All Day Long* (Harper Business, 2009), 114.

CHAPTER 9: TOO LITTLE AND TOO MUCH

1   David Rock, *Your Brain at Work: Strategies for Overcoming Distraction, Regaining Focus, and Working Smarter All Day Long* (Harper Business, 2009), 113–14; M. D. Lieberman, N. I. Eisenberger, M. J. Crockett, S. M. Tom, J. H. Pfeifer, and B. M. Way, "Putting Feelings into Words: Affect Labeling Disrupts Amygdala Activity in Response to Affective Stimuli," *Psychological Science* 18, no. 5 (2007): 421–28.

2   K. N. Ochsner, R. D. Ray, J. C. Cooper, E. R. Robertson, S. Chopra, J. D. E. Gabrieli et al., "For Better or for Worse: Neural Systems Supporting the Cognitive Down- and Up-Regulation of Negative Emotion," *Neuroimage* 23, no. 2 (2004): 483–99, https://pubmed.ncbi.nlm.nih.gov/15488398/; Rock, *Your Brain at Work*, 127.

3   S. Stepper and F. Strack, "Proprioceptive Determinants of Emotional and Nonemotional Feelings," *Journal of Personality and Social Psychology* 64, no. 2 (1993): 211–20, https://psycnet.apa.org/record/1993-20771-001; Diana Fosha, Daniel Siegel, and Marion F. Solomon, *The Healing Power of Emotion: Affective Neuroscience, Development & Clinical Practice* (Norton, 2009), 213.

4   Susan Magsamen and Ivy Ross, *Your Brain on Art: How the Arts Transform Us* (Random House, 2023).

5   John M. Gottman, *The Science of Trust: Emotional Attunement for Couples* (Norton, 2011), 20.

6   Daniel J. Siegel, *Mindsight: The New Science of Personal Transformation* (Bantam Books, 2011), 26.

7   Gottman, *The Science of Trust*, 20.

8   Gottman, *The Science of Trust*, 15.

CHAPTER 10: IMPULSES AND EXPRESSION

1   Antonio Damasio, *The Feeling of What Happens: Body and Emotion in the Making of Consciousness* (Houghton Mifflin Harcourt, 1999), 49.

2   David Rock, *Your Brain at Work: Strategies for Overcoming Distraction, Regaining Focus, and Working Smarter All Day Long* (Harper Business, 2009), 56.

3   Rock, *Your Brain at Work*, 53; Daniel Kahneman, *Thinking, Fast and Slow* (Farrar, Straus and Giroux, 2011), 42.

CHAPTER 11: ANGER

1   Thich Nhat Hanh, *Anger: Wisdom for Cooling the Flames* (Riverhead, 2001), 58–59.

PART FOUR: LEARNING AND CHANGE

1   Louis J. Cozolino, *The Neuroscience of Psychotherapy: Building and Rebuilding the Human Brain* (Norton, 2002), 209.

CHAPTER 12: HOW PEOPLE CHANGE

1   David Rock, *Your Brain at Work: Strategies for Overcoming Distraction, Regaining Focus, and Working Smarter All Day Long* (Harper Business, 2009), 151.

2   Peter Block, *The Answer to How Is Yes: Acting on What Matters* (Berrett-Koehler, 2001).

3   David Brooks, "Can You Become a Better Person by Confronting Your Worst Self?," NPR *TED Radio Hour*, June 16, 2017, https://www.npr.org/transcripts/532841680.

4   Brent J. Atkinson, *Emotional Intelligence in Couples Therapy: Advances from Neurobiology and the Science of Intimate Relationships* (Norton, 2005), 2.

5   Frans de Waal, *Mama's Last Hug: Animal Emotions and What They Tell Us About Ourselves* (Norton, 2019), 213–14.

6   De Waal, *Mama's Last Hug*, 213–14, 216.

7   Amy Novotney, "What Happens in Your Brain When You Give a Gift?," *American Psychological Association*, December 9, 2022, https://www.apa.org/topics/mental-health/brain -giftgiving#:~:text=They%20found%20that%20those%20 who,social%2Demotional%20well%2Dbeing.

CHAPTER 13: BECOMING
LEARNING PARTNERS

1   Louis J. Cozolino, *The Neuroscience of Psychotherapy: Building and Rebuilding the Human Brain* (Norton, 2002), 341.

2   Thomas Lewis, Fari Amini, and Richard Lannon, *A General Theory of Love* (Random House, 2000), 144.

3   Timothy D. Wilson, *Strangers to Ourselves: Discovering the Adaptive Unconscious* (Belknap Press, 2002), 24.

4   Frank Anthony DePhillips, William M. Berliner, and James J. Cribbin, "Meaning of Learning and Knowledge," in Management of Training Programs (Richard D. Irwin, 1960), 69.

5   Unknown source.

6   Daniel C. Dennett, *Consciousness Explained* (Little, Brown, 1991), 160–64.

7   Krista Tippett, host, *On Being with Krista Tippett*, podcast
      interview with Daniel Kahneman, "Why We Contradict
      Ourselves and Confound Each Other," 2017, https://onbeing
      .org/programs/daniel-kahneman-why-we-contradict
      -ourselves-and-confound-each-other/.
8   Robert Wright, *Why Buddhism Is True* (Simon & Schuster,
      2017); Eric Swanson and Yongey Mingyur Rinpoche, *The
      Joy of Living: Unlocking the Secret and Science of Happiness*
      (Random House, 2010), 250.

CONCLUSION: THE POETRY
OF RELATIONSHIP

1   Jane Hirshfield, *Ten Windows: How Great Poems Transform
      the World* (Alfred A. Knopf, 2015), 264.
2   Hirshfield, *Ten Windows*, 250.
3   Hirshfield, *Ten Windows*, 264.
4   Hirshfield, *Ten Windows*, 244.
5   Hirshfield, *Ten Windows*, 265.
6   Hirshfield, *Ten Windows*, 251.
7   Hirshfield, *Ten Windows*, 271.

Index

B

U

V

W

Y

About the Author

© Michael Lundgren

Kathryn Ford, MD, is a psychiatrist, couples therapist, and author. Her work is a unique integration of mindfulness, psychotherapy, and neuroscience. After receiving her MD from Brown School of Medicine, Dr. Ford completed a residency in psychiatry at Stanford University School of Medicine. She has studied and practiced meditation at centers like Barre Center for Buddhist Studies in Massachusetts and Spirit Rock Meditation Center in California, which developed her understanding of the power of mindfulness for building deeper, more resilient relationships. Originally from Texas, she raised her family and developed her work in the San Francisco Bay Area. She and her husband, Peter Finkelstein, now spend time in the Bay Area, rural Rhode Island, and Orcas Island, Washington. They have three grown children.